PITMAN'S MOTORISTS LIBRARY

THE BOOK OF THE AUSTIN SEVEN

A COMPLETE GUIDE FOR OWNERS OF ALL
MODELS WITH DETAILS OF CHANGES IN
DESIGN AND EQUIPMENT SINCE 1927

BY

GORDON G. GOODWIN

D1354244

1942

British Library Cataloguing-in-Publication Data
A catalogue record for this book is available from the
British Library

Austin 7

The Austin 7 was an economy car produced from 1922 until 1939 in the United Kingdom by the Austin Motor Company. Nicknamed the 'Baby Austin', it was one of the most popular cars ever produced for the British market, and sold well abroad. It almost completely wiped out most other British small cars and cyclecars of the early 1920s, and its effect on the British market was similar to that of the Model T Ford in the USA. It was also licensed and copied by companies all over the world. The very first BMW car, the BMW Dixi, was a licensed Austin 7, as were the original American Austins. In France they were made and sold as Rosengarts, and in Japan, Nissan also used the 7 design as the basis for their first cars, although not under licence.

Many Austin 7s were rebuilt as 'specials' after the Second World War, including the first race car built by Bruce McLaren, and the first Lotus, the Lotus Mk1, which was based on an Austin 7. Such was the power of the Austin 7 name, that the company re-used it for early versions of the A30 in 1951 and the Mini in 1959. Until the First World War Austin built mainly large cars, but in 1909 they sold a single-cylinder small car built by Swift of Coventry called the Austin 7 hp. It was a moderate success, but after this, the company returned to making larger cars.

In 1920, Sir Herbert Austin commenced working on the concept of a smaller car, mainly to meet the needs of young families aspiring to own an affordable motor car. This idea was spurred on by the introduction of the Horsepower Tax in 1921. His design concept marked a departure from his company's conservative motoring past and Austin received considerable opposition from his board of directors and creditors. However, because the company was in receivership, Austin carried out the project himself. In 1921 he hired an eighteen year old draughtsman, Stanley Edge, from the Austin factory at Longbridge, Birmingham to aid in the drawing of detailed plans.

Edge convinced Austin to use a small four-cylinder engine. The original side valve engine design featured a capacity of 696cc, giving a RAC rating of 7.2 hp, whilst the cast cylinder block featured a detachable head and was mounted on an aluminium crankcase. The crankshaft used one roller and two ball bearings and the big-ends were splash lubricated. Edge also carried out the design of other mechanical components such as the three speed gearbox and clutch assembly. Austin was largely responsible for styling the Seven's design, which was reportedly influenced by the design of the Peugeot Quadrilette. The 'A' frame chassis design was believed to have been influenced by the design of an American truck used in the Longbridge factory in the early 1920s.

The design was completed in 1922 and three prototypes were constructed in a special area of the Longbridge factory, and announced to the public in July 1922. Austin had put a large amount of his own money into the design and patented many of its innovations in his own name. In return for his investment he was paid a royalty of two guineas (£2.10) on every car sold. Nearly 2,500 cars were made in the first year of production (1923), not as many as hoped, but within a few years the 'big car in miniature' had wiped out the cyclecar industry and transformed the fortunes of the Austin Motor Company. By 1939 when production finally ended, 290,000 cars and vans had been made.

Today, these old Austins are much loved by collectors and car enthusiasts alike. The interest in these pioneers of the small and affordable automobile shows no sign of waning, and if anything, the market for vintage cars has taken an upturn of late. We hope the reader enjoys this book.

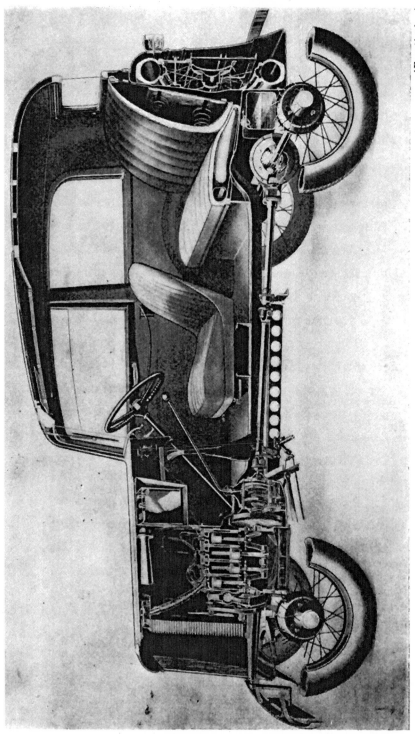

Sectional View of Austin Seven Saloon

(*Frontispiece*)

CONTENTS

THE BOOK OF
THE AUSTIN SEVEN

CHAPTER I

ACHIEVEMENT

SINCE the first Austin Seven of the present type (a single cylinder
Austin Seven was marketed as long ago as 1910) left the Austin
Motor Company's Works at Longbridge in 1922, over 250,000
have gone to Austin buyers in every country in the world.

As the "Baby" Austin it is known everywhere. Jokes have
been made, and songs composed about it. It has become a house-
hold word, not only among the English-speaking peoples but in
every land where cars are known.

This chapter will give the Austin Seven owner, actual or pro-
spective, an inkling of the capabilities of this staunch little car.
The feats described are the more impressive when it is realized
that they were performed by Austin Sevens the same in every
respect as the thousands of others in active service on the highways and byways of the world.

The Austin Seven has travelled to places hitherto inaccessible
to motorists, many of which have not since been reached by car.
It has several times been round the world, made numerous
record transcontinental journeys, crossed deserts, climbed mountains, traversed equatorial forests, and even participated in polar
expeditions. It has climbed Ben Nevis, Galdhopiggen—Norway's
highest peak, Table Mountain, and in the mountains of the
Himalayas has reached altitudes higher than any other car has
yet attempted.

A number of notabilities and royalties have purchased Austin
Sevens, including the Grand Llama of Tibet. Roads are non-
existent in the Forbidden Land, being merely mule tracks, in
many places as many as twenty running alongside one another.
Great difficulty was experienced in getting the Llama's car into
Tibet owing to the inaccessibility of that strange country. The
car had to be dismantled and transported in parts over 200 miles,
by either pack-mule or coolie, and reassembled at the other end.

Mention must be made of the gallant effort in 1928 of two

1

New Zealanders—Hector Macquarrie and Richard Matthews, who were seized with the ambition to be the first to take a car overland from Sydney to Cape York through the tropical bush of Northern Queensland, Australia.

This task was duly accomplished and a new memorial set up to the reliability of Austin products.

More recently these two adventurers have travelled round the

FIG. 1. THE SEVEN BREAKING CROSS-COUNTRY RECORDS IN NEW ZEALAND

world in their Austin Seven, an epic circular tour that is a glowing testimony of this wonderful little car's reliability.

The Austin Seven that ascended Table Mountain accomplished the deed in 10¾ hours and climbed 3,300 ft. along paths which no car had previously traversed. The journey was a motoring nightmare, a wild scramble over bushes and boulders.

The members of the expedition were Mr. Ronald F. Jones, who drove the car, Mr. Kenneth Campbell of the Mountain Club of South Africa, Mr. B. Mansfield, and Mr. Cartwright, a representative of the Cape *Argus*.

Mr. Jones changed down after the first hundred yards of the

ascent and for the rest of the day the car was never out of bottom gear. The lower granite slopes of the famous Mountain gave the little car a rough and strenuous time.

In May, 1929, Miss Gladys de Havilland completed her round-the-world tour in her Austin Seven which was commenced from the Midlands in October, 1928.

The American people were immensely tickled that a woman

FIG. 2. THE AUSTIN SEVEN THAT MACQUARRIE AND MATTHEWS DROVE ROUND THE WORLD IS SHOWN HERE ON A ROAD IN YUGOSLAVIA

should attempt such a journey in a "toy auto." They realized its merit, however, when despite adverse conditions and difficulties associated with the winter season on the American Continent, Miss de Havilland managed to reach New York from San Francisco, in good time and without any trouble.

Its known ability to perform well under extremely adverse conditions was undoubtedly the reason for the inclusion of an Austin Seven in the equipment of the Wilkins-Byrd Antarctic Expedition which took place in 1930.

The terribly arduous conditions, including snowstorms and

blizzards, did not prevent the Austin Seven from giving of its best. The rigorous conditions imposed by an expedition into the Antarctic wastes where temperature is many degrees below zero, provide an exhausting test for any motor-car. The Austin Seven used in this expedition gave such yeoman service that Sir Hubert Wilkins again chose this staunch little car as his mobile auxiliary on his more recent Ellsworth Antarctic expedition.

FIG. 3. TABLE MOUNTAIN WAS CONQUERED BY THIS AUSTIN SEVEN IN 10¾ HOURS, CLIMBING 3,300 FT.

Mr. Cederwall-Larsen chose an Austin Seven for his attempt to scale Galdhopiggen, Northern Europe's highest peak, 8,000 ft. above sea level. Mr. Cederwall-Larsen anticipated that his attempt to scale Norway's highest peak would take no more than two days. It took the whole of one day, however, to get quite a short distance from Oslo to the Seter.

The venture was resumed at five-o'clock the next morning, but shortly afterwards the little Seven with its trailer had plunged into a ravine filled with loose snow. On the face of it the position appeared hopeless, but by dint of two days' labour the car was restored to firm ice ready for the climb up the mountain slope.

The expedition was fated not to start yet. A snowstorm sprang up and blew for eleven days. During the lulls the party were able to dig the Baby Austin and its trailer free from snow, and when the storm eventually abated the upward climb was resumed, and three weeks after leaving Oslo the actual climb of Galdhopiggen was begun.

The difficulties, which were many, included the "Piggebreen" glacier, which had to be surmounted somehow. It was found impossible to cut a path for the Austin Seven in the solid ice of the glacier, so it was decided to build a ramp of snow which was stamped down hard. This took the party three further days of hard work. Eventually after overcoming many difficulties, the party managed to get within a short distance of the cairn at the summit.

The final stage of the climb was left till the next day, but overnight a violent snowstorm blew up, fiercer than any that had been met with since they left Oslo.

The hut in which the little party slept that night (slept, that is, until the storm arose) was situated a little farther down the mountain than their car, and when the hut started to rock in the fury of the elements, they feared that the car would be blown down on top of them. Fortunately, their fears did not materialize, but when, after the storm had ceased, they made their way up to their Austin Seven, they found it covered with ice and snow.

After some considerable time spent digging the snow away they were eventually able to lift the bonnet, to discover that the fine snow particles had been driven in between the bonnet louvres and other openings until the under-bonnet space was packed solid. The engine was eventually cleared and the carburettor, coil, ignition leads, plugs, etc., cleaned as well as could be done under the circumstances. The ignition was switched on, the starting handle turned, and much to the surprise of the party the engine started up as usual. They were then able finally to conquer the summit of Galdhopiggen, which they did about noon on Ascension Day.

Mr. L. H. Dupuis and the Maharaj Emur of Burdwan, with an Austin Seven surmounted Sandakphu, a mountain in the Himalayas over 12,000 ft. above sea level. The circumstances of this climb were extremely arduous, the first 10,000 ft. of altitude including many hair-pin bends and adverse gradients. The final fourteen miles were the worst, the mountain track being no wider than the Seven in many places. It was composed of innumerable zigzag bends often so acute as to require the help of natives in their negotiation, with the mountain rock on the one side and a clean drop over a precipice on the other.

Crowbars had to be used, at one part of the climb, where the mountain rock encroached on the path to such an extent as to prevent the passage of the little Seven. Eventually the path was widened sufficiently to allow the car to pass. The number of severely zigzag turns increased as the climb progressed. One was encountered with such an acute bend that, with a precipice so close, it was found impossible to turn the car. It had to be manhandled up on to the higher track and driven in reverse gear until sufficient room was found in which to turn the car by lifting, so that it faced forward in the way it should go. The summit was eventually reached after innumerable difficulties had been triumphantly overcome.

Since this feat was accomplished Mr. Dupuis and the Austin Seven accompanied by Mr. C. E. Dudley, General Secretary to the Maharaj of Sikkim, have succeeded in reaching the summit of the Nathu-La Pass. As on the Sandakphu venture the mountain path was often very little wider than the car, and series of zigzag bends were met. Such a series was encountered at the outset, the lowest part of which had been carried away in a landslide, necessitating a climb up a steep slope with a gradient of 1 in 2 to the next leg of the track. Hair-pin bends with gradients of 1 in 2½ were the kind of obstacle encountered. One particularly bad spot was a badly surfaced climb of 2½ miles, the gradient ranging between 1 in 2 to 1 in 5. The first day's climb brought the party to an altitude of 9,000 ft. at Rarponag Bungalow where the night was passed.

The next day saw the party on their way again, but the venture was nearly terminated in an abrupt fashion. The car was climbing up the narrow mountain track with the ever-present precipice on the one side, when the outermost rear wheel slipped over the edge. The driver saved the situation in the nick of time by promptly accelerating, thereby regaining the path. Further on, conditions improved, until at about 12 miles from the start a rock outcrop restricted the path to less than the width of the car. The rock was too formidable to warrant attack by crowbars, so the track had to be widened by building it out. The drop at this point was 600 ft., proof of the faith the party had in their road engineering efforts.

Another landslide, or rather the results of one, met the adventurers two miles farther on. The road had completely disappeared. Road construction was again the order of the day and it was three days before the party was again able to proceed. Changu Bungalow, close to the Changu Lake, where the mountaineers stayed for a night, was reached after crossing a flimsy

FIG. 4. THIS AUSTIN SEVEN HAD TO TRAVERSE NARROW MOUNTAIN TRACKS WHEN IT SURMOUNTED THE CREST OF THE NATHU-LA IN THE HIMALAYAS, 14,780 FT. ABOVE SEA-LEVEL

bridge over a mountain torrent with only an inch and a half to spare on either side.

The last section of the climb up to the crest of the Nathu-La was the most severe of all, necessitating the fitting of chains before the summit was reached at an altitude of 14,780 ft. above sea-level. This is probably the highest altitude ever attained by a car driven by its own power.

The return journey down the mountain was just as dangerous as the ascent, perhaps it may be considered more so when the narrow mountain track had to be traversed after dark by the aid of the lights on the car.

The accomplishment stands out as the more remarkable when it is realized that the engine is only developing half its available power at this altitude owing to the effect of the rarefaction of the atmosphere on the carburation.

No special preparations were taken as regards the Austin Seven beyond taking off its silencer, although it had already travelled 60,000 miles.

SPECIFICATION OF MODELS

General. Since the conception of the first single-cylinder Austin Seven, the name Austin has been coupled with light cars. The

FIG. 5. THE AUSTIN SEVEN PEARL CABRIOLET

most famous of all baby cars, the Austin Seven has gone from success to success, more than 250,000 having passed into the hands of owners whose praise has built up a reputation second to none. It is now more than thirteen years since the first Austin Seven of the present type left the Austin Works at Longbridge. Since this happy event, its value has increased with each successive year, until we now have a large car in miniature, capable of transporting four adults long distances in comfort, with a specification undreamt of twelve years ago, and available to the public at half the cost of its venerable ancestor.

The latest models possess many striking improvements, and the Ruby Saloon and Pearl Cabriolet of the present range are the most elegant small cars on the market. These two models have

Fig. 6. The 1937 Series Austin Seven Ruby Saloon

Fig. 7. The Improved Frontal Aspect of the New Seven

bodies of pleasing design incorporating a new radiator design which breaks away from the old upright Austin style. The latest cellulosed radiator cowl is tasteful and dignified; it slopes back slightly, is nicely rounded, and merges cleanly into the sweeping lines of the longer bonnet. The frontal aspect of the new Seven is also improved by curved fairings and new wings.

PRICES OF MODELS

Ruby Saloon	£125
Ruby Fixed Head Saloon . .	£118
Pearl Cabriolet	£128
Open Road Tourer . . .	£112
Two-seater . . .	£102 10s.
Nippy Sports	£142
Nippy Sports with Standard Engine	£130

The Austin Seven chassis frame has always been notable by reason of its strong triangulated design, but these latest bodies are now mounted on a newly designed, low-dropped frame. By so doing the Saloons and Cabriolet now possess a floor level 5 in. lower than formerly, at the same time providing ample foot room for the rear passengers, without the use of foot wells.

The lower body mounting, involving a lower centre of gravity, and larger tyres have together been responsible for a marked improvement in all-round road-holding and steering qualities.

The low flat floor, wide doors, and tip-up front seats give easy access to the rear compartment. The pneumatic upholstery is trimmed in good quality leather and the front seats are readily adjustable. The battery is now much more accessibly positioned. It is mounted, like the tool-box, under the bonnet in front of the scuttle where attention can be paid to it without disturbing the seat. The downswept tail of the car contains a spare wheel compartment and it also houses the luggage carrier when the latter is not in use.

This low frame chassis is the first Austin Seven chassis incorporating a luggage carrier, which, although of light construction, is well able to take luggage up to ½ cwt. in weight and can be easily and neatly stowed away behind the spare wheel cover. The Saloon and Cabriolet are well ventilated, apart from the facilities provided by the windscreen and winding door-windows, by the door type louvres and special rear quarter windows which open at the trailing edges to ensure adequate ventilation. The new Ruby Saloon has winding rear windows.

The Ruby Saloon de Luxe has a single fastening sunshine roof that can be secured in any position, and the Pearl Cabriolet head also can be secured in a half-open position if desired.

Although the convertible head of this model is of a fabric

material the same type of rear quarter window as described on the Ruby Saloon ensures efficient ventilation on the Cabriolet when the head is in the fully shut position.

To lower the special type of roof on the Austin Seven Pearl Cabriolet, the following procedure is necessary. Release the two fastenings above the windscreen (one is shown at *A* in 1, Fig. 14) and lift the canopy rod. Then detach the three clips which secure

FIG. 8. THE CURVED DOWNSWEPT REAR PANEL OF THE SEVEN

the front bar on which the fabric is carried. Roll back the fabric as far as it will go and secure the roll (as in 2, Fig. 14) by fastening the loop provided at each side to the top stud of each roof stretcher (as at *B*) then swing forward the hinged roof-bar (*E*). Pull the two arms (*C* and *D*) of each roof stretcher in the direction of the arrows to break the joint, fold the rear portion of the hood down (3, Fig. 14) and secure the rear window by its two straps to the fastenings on the top of the folded roof member. The roof stretcher joints must not be broken before the front of the roof fabric is released from the canopy rod.

Raising the roof is a reversal of the above operations. In lifting the roof members to the door pillars ensure that the locating dowel enters the hole in each pillar (as at *F* and *G* in 3, Fig. 14). The roof can be left rolled back at the partially open position shown in 2 Fig. 14 if desired.

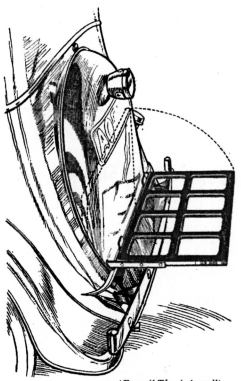

FIG. 9. SHOWING HOW THE LUGGAGE CARRIER
FOLDS AWAY INSIDE THE REAR PANEL

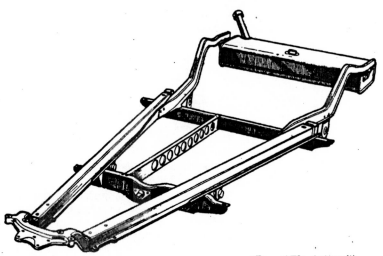

FIG. 10. THE NEW LOW FRAME OF THE SEVEN

The fascia boards of the closed models are attractive and practical. A capacious cubby hole for parcels, etc., forms the nearside of the instrument panel and so conforms with Austin practice on the larger models. All the instruments are sensibly and tastefully grouped immediately in front of the driver and are illuminated indirectly so that no glare can dazzle at night.

The speedometer is interesting in that it is of the new magnetic

(From " The Autocar ")

FIG. 11. THE TRAFFICATORS ARE FITTED IN
THE DOOR PILLARS

type in which the figures of the mileage recording part of the instrument are carried on drums instead of discs.

The system is ingenious; the drive rotates a small permanent magnet setting up eddy currents that cause an aluminium disc to rotate. The disc is connected to the pointer, which is tensioned by a spring. The greater the speed of rotation the greater is the dragging effect of the eddy currents from the magnet, so that a steady and accurate reading is given.

Ease of control is a prominent safety feature of the new Sevens, both the throttle and ignition controls having disappeared from the steering. The control of the ignition is now attended to by

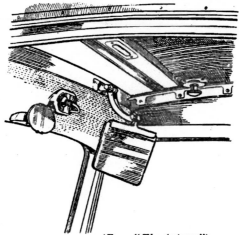

(*From " The Autocar"*)

FIG. 12. THE SUNSHINE ROOF, ELECTRIC WINDSCREEN
WIPER, AND SUN VISOR ON THE NEW SEVEN

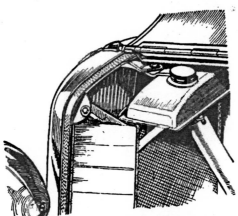

(*From " The Autocar"*)

FIG. 13. THE RADIATOR FILLER CAP IS
SITUATED UNDER THE BONNET

an automatic centrifugally operated mechanism in the distributor head which relieves the driver of the necessity of constant adjustment of a hand control. Its advantages are most evident when accelerating, etc., as the ignition is advanced in proportion to the engine speed. The throttle is now connected to the air strangler control and the headlamps are of the dip and switch type with separate side- or parking-lamps. The dipped beam is controlled by a switch mounted on the toe-plate inside the car

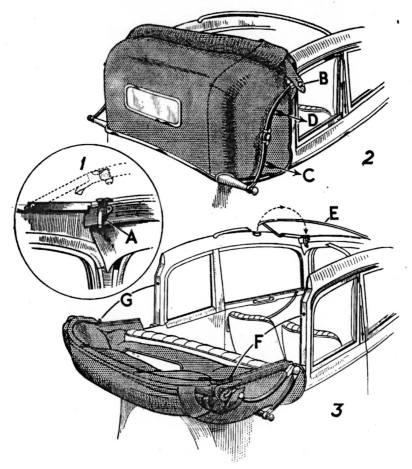

FIG. 14. SHOWING HOW THE SPECIAL TYPE ROOF IS LOWERED
ON THE PEARL CABRIOLET

to the left of the clutch pedal and is operated by a single movement of the foot. The direction indicators, too, have an automatic action; they return to their recesses in the door pillars upon the reverse action of the steering wheel, i.e. when the car is straightened up after a turn or a manoeuvre.

The Open Road tourer and the two-seater are mounted on the new low frame. Their specification includes the four-speed gearbox with synchromesh for second, third and top and the safety features: automatic advance and retard mechanism for the ignition, combined throttle and strangler control, automatic return direction-indicators, and the five lamp set with foot controlled dip-and-switch headlamps. The upholstery is pneumatic and trimmed in good quality leather-cloth. The open two-seater will carry a considerable amount of luggage at the rear of the tip-up front seats and the hood and side-curtains of both the two-seater and the four-seater tourer can be rapidly erected or stowed away, and when up, give the occupants complete protection from the most inclement weather.

The hoods and side curtains of these open cars will benefit from a little care in the handling of them. If the car has seen hard service the usual faded appearance of the hood can easily be remedied by a good clean with a brush and cold water. When the hood has dried apply a good quality black boot polish with a brush and rub it in well, especially round the hood seams, in order to fill the stitch holes and make them waterproof. If this is done and followed with a brisk rub the appearance of the hood will be considerably enhanced.

To lower the hood, first release it from the pillars of the windscreen and push the side screens inwards so that their rubber buffers clear the iron framework.

Then push the hood straight up and back from the front and break the joints.

The hood will then collapse towards the back of the car. Pull the material out until it lies in one big fold over the back of the car; fix the hood frame to the hood rest on the body by means of the fasteners on the strap at the front end of the hood, and secure the two rear window fasteners on to their two studs at the back of the body. If the hood cover is used, then the two straps on the hood cover will clip on to these two studs instead.

Then fold the hood material back, ensuring that the edges are even, turn them in, and fit the cover over.

Complete the job by securing the cover by the straps, one on each side.

When it is desired to raise the hood, remove the cover, release the clip, and unfold the hood material. Lift the top hood stick vertically, holding the metal side-iron of the hood frame near the hinge. Push the front hood stick forward and pull back the irons to straighten the hinge and the whole hood can be dropped forward and secured in position to the windscreen.

Correct stowing of the side curtains is important if they are to

FIG. 15. THE AUSTIN SEVEN OPEN ROAD TOURER

FIG. 16. THE AUSTIN SEVEN TWO-SEATER

enjoy a long life; celluloid is easily scratched and becomes brittle as it ages.

It is a good plan to wrap them in some protective material to prevent them from rubbing together and chafing with the motion of the car.

On the 1935 Open Road Tourer the side-curtains are stowed away behind the rear seat squab, which can be hinged forward

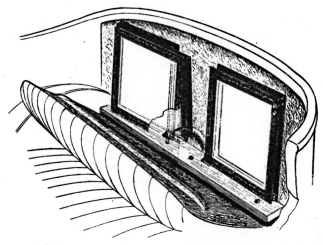

Fig. 17. The Side Curtains of the 1935 Four-seaters are Safely Stowed Away behind the Rear-seat Squab

revealing the wood base into which they can be secured. The rear curtains should be dealt with first, their pegs fitting into suitably positioned slots on each side of the spare wheel carrier pressing. Round holes accommodate the front curtains. Care should be taken to ensure that the side curtains from each side of the car are stowed on the same side in the recess with all hinges next to the body sides. On the latest tourers the side curtains are stowed in the door panels.

The Nippy and Speedy Sports models vary in specification from the standard cars. Apart from the bodies and the engine the chief chassis difference is in the suspension.

The front axle beam has a definite drop so that the slightly curved, semi-elliptic transverse spring is considerably lower although still above the axle beam. The road springs, front and rear, are taped and friction type shock absorbers are used.

Considering the engine, the cylinder block and the cylinder head are chromidium castings, the cylinder head being of an improved design giving a high compression ratio and with the combustion spaces well over the valves. The sparking plugs are centred over the valves instead of being over the pistons as in the standard engine. The tulip valves with double springs are operated by a high-lift camshaft; the carburettor is of Zenith manufacture and is of the downdraught type.

On the Nippy the lubrication system is slightly modified. The crankshaft is even more robust, is machined all over, and the

FIG. 18. THE AUSTIN SEVEN NIPPY TWO-SEATER SPORTS

big end bearings are larger. The oil passages inside the crankshaft also are slightly different.

The lubrication system on the Speedy is quite different. Here, there is a forced feed system with a pressure of about 50 lb. per sq. in. under normal working conditions. The ball and roller crankshaft bearings are lubricated by splash like the other models but the connecting rod big ends and the camshaft get the full pressure feed.

The oil is forced from the pump through channels cast in the crankcase and then through a pipe into a chamber in the crankcase front cover. The oil is retained in this chamber by a leather washer between a face on the front of the crankcase and a flange on the starting handle shaft. The pressure of the oil keeps this joint oil-tight. The oil passes through the starting dog into the front end of the hollow crankshaft and from there is forced to the four connecting rod bearings. Both Nippy and Speedy are fitted with a double capacity (1 gallon) sump with deep cooling fins.

Like the crankshaft the steel connecting rods are machined all over and oil holes lead oil to the gudgeon pins which are fully floating with aluminium end pads to prevent scoring of the cylinders. Other features include a radiator stone guard, a spring spoked steering wheel, and a Burgess silencer. The Speedy includes among its instruments a 5 in. combined speedometer and revolution counter and a quick-action filler cap is supplied

FIG. 19. THE AUSTIN SEVEN SPEEDY TWO-SEATER SPORTS
(This model is no longer marketed)

for the 12 gallon rear petrol tank; its windscreen, headlamps and mudguards can be dismantled for competition work. The engine of the discontinued Speedy model is now incorporated in the Nippy chassis.

A practical feature of the Nippy model is the hinged rear panel that conceals the spare wheel, the pump, wheel brace, jack and jack handle. These tools are all firmly fixed in position and enable a wheel to be changed without opening the bonnet to get the tools from the special compartment forward of the scuttle. The luggage space is separated from this spare wheel compartment and can be reached from inside the body behind the two adjustable tip-up front seats. The windscreen of the Nippy is a single panel one and can be hinged upwards. The Speedy windscreen is of the vee-type. The hoods of both models can be rapidly erected and stowed away. The following instructions for folding the hood apply to the Nippy Seven. (See 1, 2 and 3, Fig. 20.)

The first operation is to release the press stud fasteners that secure the bottom of the hood to the body; there are eight in all. Then release the front hood rail from the windscreen pillars by unscrewing the two finger nuts (incidentally these should subsequently be screwed up again to prevent rattle). The hood material being free, lay it over the tail of the body, tilt the seats forward.

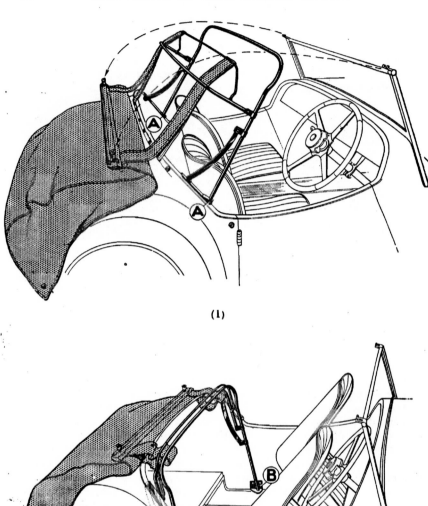

(1)

(2)

FIG. 20. SHOWING HOW THE HOOD IS FOLDED ON THE NIPPY SEVEN

pull the main hood iron out of its sockets *A* (Fig. 20) in the body and swing it down to fit in the sockets in the floor *B* (Fig. 20). This also serves to close the hood frame. Turning to the hood material and working from the back of the car, fold both rear corners well under and roll from the bottom edge up under the rear window, until all the material can be tucked between the

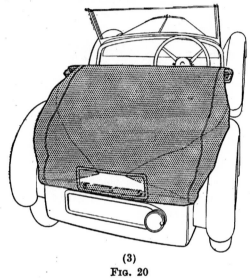

(3)

Fig. 20

body and the hood frame. The hood cover can then be drawn into position to complete the job.

Engine. The four-cylinder water-cooled engine has a bore and stroke of 56 × 76 millimetres, giving a capacity of 747 cubic centimetres. The R.A.C. rating is 7·8 h.p. and the tax £6. 13·5 b.h.p. is developed by the two-bearing engine at 3,000 r.p.m. The new three-bearing engine develops 17 b.h.p. at 3,800 r.p.m. The Nippy Sports engine develops 20 b.h.p. at 4,000 r.p.m., and the Speedy engine 23 at 4,800 r.p.m. Oil consumption is approximately 1,000 to 1,200 m.p.g. Petrol consumption is about 45 m.p.g. at 30 m.p.h. Petrol consumption of the Sports models is much the same as the standard cars at touring speeds.

The cast-iron cylinder block is bolted to an aluminium crankcase which is closed at the base by a sump cover. The engine feet are rubber-mounted to absorb vibration.

The design of the engine is simplicity itself, it being only necessary to undo the water outlet branch (one setscrew) and disconnect the sparking-plug leads before removing the detachable cylinder head for decarbonizing. The side valves are all on the nearside and are operated from the camshaft by adjustable tappets.

The valve chest is enclosed by an oil-tight cover secured with two knurled screws. The crankshaft is robust and is carried on ball and roller bearings, the pistons are of low-expansion aluminium alloy and the exhaust and inlet manifolds are cast in one to provide a hot spot. The latest engine has its crankshaft carried in a third main bearing which is of the plain or shell type. The connecting rods are of steel and the gudgeon pins are clamped in. The lower of three piston rings on each piston scrapes down the surplus oil that has been flung up by the crankshaft, and returns it to the sump, which holds half a gallon, after passing through the filter gauze above the sump cover. Engine lubrication is by means of a mechanical vane pump which is driven by skew gearing from the camshaft and which forces the oil to the rear camshaft bearing, to the oil pressure gauge on the instrument board, and then along the crankcase to supply the two jets that point downwards into the interior of the crankcase. From these two jets the oil falls on to the crankshaft throws as the crankshaft revolves under the jets. The throws have pockets machined there for the purpose of catching the oil from the jets and passing it on to lubricate the main and big-end bearings. The latest engine addition incorporates a special pressure feed to the middle crankshaft and camshaft bearing.

Chassis lubrication is by grease gun. Cooling is by thermosiphon and fan, the fan being driven by belt from a fan pulley on the camshaft. Ignition is by battery and coil and the Zenith carburettor is supplied with petrol from the 5 gallon petrol tank at the rear by an A.C. petrol pump operated by an eccentric on the camshaft. The carburettor embodies the well known Zenith principles of main and compensating jets, and is noted for its absence of moving parts. The petrol pump always supplies the correct amount of fuel as required by the carburettor. An automatic mechanism governs the supply and meters it out correctly.

Clutch. The clutch is of the single dry-plate type, with a central sprung plate, very light in operation and smooth in taking up the drive. Lubrication of the clutch is dealt with on page 51 and clutch relining instructions on page 78.

Gearbox and Transmission. The four-speed gearbox is rigidly bolted to the engine and contains 1½ pints of lubricant. Gear changes are readily and silently effected by a long central gear lever easily reached by the driver. Changes into second, third and top gears are facilitated by the synchromesh mechanism. The ratios provided by the gearbox between the engine and the road wheels are: 1st, 22·94 to 1, 2nd, 13·85 to 1; 3rd, 8·73 to 1 and top 5·25 to 1. On the Nippy Sports the ratios are 21·9 to 1, 13·3 to 1, 8·38 to 1, and 5·6 to 1. On the Speedy they were 20·48 to 1, 12·39 to 1, 7·82 to 1, and 5·25 to 1.

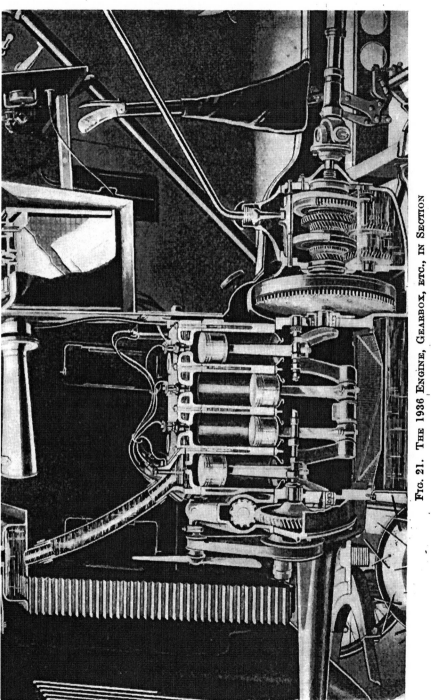

Fig. 21. The 1936 Engine, Gearbox, etc., in Section

The rear axle is of the spiral bevel three-quarter floating type with di*erential and torque tube. The universal joints of the propeller shaft have needle bearings front and rear on the low frame chassis.

These new needle roller bearings have a large number of small diameter rollers that have a very long life. The universals are charged with lubricant during manufacture and require no

FIG. 22. THE FRONT UNIVERSAL JOINT WITH NEEDLE BEARINGS

further attention. Actually they do not require oil for lubrication purposes but purely as a means of preventing corrosion.

Brakes. The hand and foot controls both operate the four-wheel brakes which are of the internal expanding type. The brakes are smooth and powerful and can be easily and independently adjusted. The brake shoes are of aluminium and relining instructions appear on page 87. The 1937 series cars have steel brake shoes and Girling type adjusters.

Steering. The steering is light and responsive and suitably raked. The steering gear is of the worm and worm-wheel type with provision for taking up wear, and provides a turning circle of 38 ft. 2 in. in diameter. The horn button is in the centre of the steering wheel, in the hub of which is located the automatic mechanism for returning the direction indicators.

Suspension. The transverse front spring is semi-elliptic, those at the rear are quarter-elliptic. Shock absorbers at front and rear are of the friction type and damp out all road shocks.

Wheels and Tyres. The wheels are of a special wire type with stainless steel centres, and can be rapidly detached without removing the securing nuts. To detach the wheel from the hub loosen the three wheel nuts *A* (Fig. 23) with the wheel brace and pull the wheel outwards about ¼ in., and a little to the left so that the large holes in the wheel centre will pass over the nuts. The wheel can then be pulled off the hub. When refitting the wheels ensure that the large holes in the wheel centre fit properly over

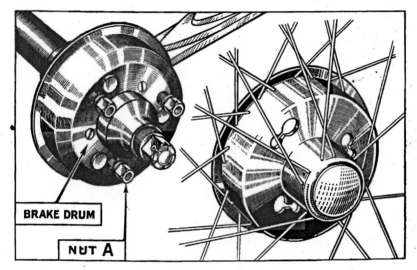

BRAKE DRUM

NUT A

FIG. 23. WHEEL DETAILS

the dowels on the hubs before tightening the wheel nuts. The tyres fitted to the "Ruby" saloons, "Pearl" cabriolet and open tourers are 4·00–17 (4·75–16 for export); the Nippy Sports model is supplied with 3·50–19 tyres.

Equipment. The equipment includes 6 volt lighting and starting with hand-starter switch, carpets, pedal rubbers, chromium plated lamps (black with chromium rims on the fixed head Ruby Saloon) dip-and-switch foot control, side lamps, direction indicators with automatic return, interior visor and luggage carrier on the Ruby de luxe Saloon and the Pearl cabriolet, rear window blind, driving mirror, draught and fume excluders, combined stop and tail lamp, bumpers front and rear on the Ruby saloon de luxe and the Pearl cabriolet, combined carburettor air strangler and throttle control, electric petrol gauge, speedometer, electric windscreen wiper, electric horn, spare wheel and tyre, number plates and licence holder.

Tools. The following is a list of the tools and extra items such as valve lifter, hub extractor, etc., which will enable the Austin

Seven owner to maintain his car in good running order. They are suitably wrapped and are kept in a special compartment.

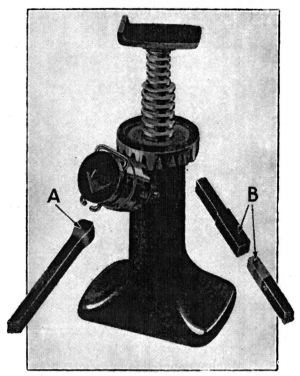

FIG. 24. THE NEW TYPE OF JACK WITH SPECIAL LIFTING PAD

A is universal end.   *B* is joint of jack handle.

Double ended spanner, $\frac{7}{16}$ in. $\times$ $\frac{1}{2}$ in.
Double ended spanner, $\frac{5}{16}$ in. $\times$ $\frac{3}{8}$ in.
Double ended spanner, $\frac{3}{16}$ in. $\times$ $\frac{1}{4}$ in.
Sparking plug box spanner.
Tommy bar.
Carburettor jet key (required for Van only).
Contact breaker spanner.

Sparking plug and tappet clearance gauge.
Tappet adjustment spanner.
Screwdriver.
Tyre levers.
4 in. adjustable spanner.
$\frac{3}{16}$ in. × $\frac{1}{4}$ in. box spanner.
$\frac{5}{16}$ in. × $\frac{3}{8}$ in. box spanner.
Tool wrap for all the above items.

The following are in addition to those in the Tool Wrap—

$\frac{5}{16}$ in. × $\frac{1}{2}$ in. box spanner.
Hub cap and steering column socket spanner.
Wheel brace.
Valve lifter.
Tyre pump.
Lifting jack.
Hub extractor.
Combination pliers.
Grease gun "Auto-Lub" type.
Spanner for dynamo casing nut and cylinder nut.
Cylinder head joint washer.
Cylinder head lifting screws.
Spanner for thrust adjusting nuts.
Two radiator hose clips.
One extra ignition key.
A spare cylinder-head joint washer is also supplied.
Extra with sports models: Valve grinding tool, special valve lifter.

DATA AND EQUIPMENT

Model	Net Weight			Overall Measurements			Ground Clearance
	cwt.	qr.	lb.	Length	Width	Height	
Ruby Saloon	12	0	14	10 ft. 7 in.	4 ft. 3 in.	5 ft. 3 in.	Low frame 6⅜ in. (1) Export 7⅝ in.
Ruby Fixed Head Saloon	12	0	0	10 ft. 3 in.	4 ft. 3 in.	5 ft. 3 in.	
Pearl Cabriolet	12	0	0	10 ft. 7 in.	4 ft. 3 in.	5 ft. 3 in.	
Open Road Tourer	10	3	0	10 ft. 3 in.	4 ft. 3 in.	5 ft. 2 in.	
Two-seater	10	0	7	10 ft. 3 in.	4 ft. 3 in.	5 ft. 1 in.	
Nippy Sports	9	3	14	9 ft. 10 in.	4 ft. 1½ in.	4 ft. 4 in.	

DATA AND EQUIPMENT (Contd.)

Model	Road Speeds at 1000 r.p.m.				Gear Ratios				Wheel Base	Track
	Top	3rd	2nd	1st	Top	3rd	2nd	1st		
Seven	14·4	8·66	5·46	3·29	5·25	8·73	13·85	22·94	6 ft. 9 in. 2057 mm.	Front— 3 ft. 4 in. 1016 mm. Rear— 3 ft. 7 in. 1092 mm.
Nippy Sports	13·44	9·02	5·69	3·29	5·6	8·38	13·3	21·9		

UPHOLSTERY

* Indicates the equipment included with each model.

Model	Choice of Austin Colours	Best Selected Hide	Leather	Leather Cloth	Mohair
Ruby Saloon . . .	1, 2, 3, 4, 9	*	—	—	—
Ruby Fixed Head Saloon .	1, 2, 3	—	†	‡	*
Pearl Cabriolet . .	1, 3, 4, 6	*	—	—	—
Open Road Tourer . .	1, 5, 9	—	—	*	—
Two-seater . . .	1, 5, 9	—	—	*	—
Nippy Sports . . .	3, 6, 7, 8	*	—	•	—

1. Royal Blue. 2. Maroon. 3. Black. 4. Westminster Green. 5. Auto Brown.
6. Cherry Red. 7. Turquoise Blue. 8. Primrose. 9. Ash Grey.

† Seats and squabs only.   ‡ Interior panels, etc.

BODY

* Indicates the equipment included with each model.

Model	Interior Visor	Spare Wheel Cover	Auto. Release Direction Indicators	Spare Wheel Comp.	Windscreen Wiper	Driving Mirror	Triplex Glass
Ruby Saloon	*	—	*	*	*	*	*
Ruby Fixed Head Saloon	—	—	*	*	*	*	*
Pearl Cabriolet	*	—	*	*	*	*	*
Open Road Tourer	*	—	*	*	*	*	*
Two-seater	—	*	*	—	*	*	*
Nippy Sports	—	—	*	*	*	*	*

CHASSIS

* Indicates the equipment included with each model.

Model	Chromium Lamps	Black Lamps Chromium Rims	Foot-operated Dip and Switch	Stop Light	Bumpers
Ruby Saloon . . .	*	—	*	*	*
Ruby Fixed Head Saloon .	—	*	*	*	—
Pearl Cabriolet . .	*	—	*	*	*
Open Road Tourer . .	*	—	*	*	—
Two-seater . . .	*	—	*	*	—
Nippy Sports . . .	*	—	*	*	—

CHASSIS (*Contd.*)

* Indicates the equipment included with each model.

Model	Electric Petrol Gauge	Speedometer	Electric Horn	Luggage Carrier	Number Plates	Spare Wheel and Tyre
Ruby Saloon . . .	*	*	*	*	*	*
Ruby Fixed Head Saloon .	*	*	*	*	*	*
Pearl Cabriolet . . .	*	*	*	*	*	*
Open Road Tourer . .	*	*	*	—	*	*
Two-seater . . .	*	*	*	—	*	*
Nippy Sports . . .	*	*	*	—	*	*

CHAPTER III

RUNNING ADJUSTMENTS

AMONG the first of the attentions that should be paid to the new car is that of tightening the cylinder head nuts. These are, of course, tight enough when the car leaves the works, but the effect of the heat developed by the engine and the bedding down of the new cylinder head gasket often permits the head nuts to be tightened quite appreciably later on. When tightening these nuts do so in the same order as specified on replacing the cylinder head after decarbonizing (see Fig. 49). The correct order is to start with the centre ones, then the corner ones, those alternately opposite and so on until all are tight. The nuts should not be tightened down hard individually. The tightening must be done gradually, the idea being to pull the cylinder head down on to the joint washer with an even pressure distributed over the whole of the joint surface. If pressure is applied more to one part than to another the joint will not be good and the head may be strained out of truth. If the cylinder head nuts are not thus tightened and get slack, either gas or water leaks may develop. The latter is particularly undesirable as a considerable leak from the cooling system into the cylinders may entail an expensive bill for repairs, water being, practically speaking, incompressible. Therefore, see to it that all cylinder head nuts and sparking plugs are tight, for even a small gas leak will mean loss of compression and impaired engine efficiency.

The wheel nuts should be checked for tightness and also the road spring clips. These are not trivial attentions for the purely fussy owner; they will assure every owner's peace of mind if properly carried out.

Periodical examination is required by the torque tube and radius rod anchorages, any slack movement found being taken up by the means of adjustment provided.

The radius rod ball-and-pin anchorage is just below the gearbox in front of the first cross member. The torque tube anchorage at the rear end of the propeller shaft has a screw adjustment which must be kept correctly adjusted. If a bumping noise is heard at the rear of the car when the drive is taken up, either when starting or accelerating when under way, it will be found that the torque tube anchorage is slack. If this state of affairs is allowed to continue the result may be a fractured anchorage.

The front shock absorbers are adjustable. Tightening the

centre nuts increases their resistance to movement, but do not overtighten as this will render the suspension harsh and jerky.

If the car bounces too much, give the centre nut a turn and try the effect before increasing the adjustment further.

The brakes on the Austin Seven are easily adjusted. The hand brake lever and the pedal are interconnected but each has a separate adjustment for taking up wear (see Fig. 25).

The hand lever and pedal of the new car will be found, like the clutch pedal, to possess a certain amount of free movement. This free movement will increase as the brake linings wear until it is found that the pedal will go down quite an appreciable amount before the brakes come on. Adjustment of these controls should be made before the free movement becomes excessive. The hand brake adjustment is by a wing nut to be found underneath the centre of the car on the brake cross shaft. Place the car on level ground and let the hand lever right off. Then turn the wing nut in a clockwise direction until the lever has only one notch of free movement. The wing nut is spring-loaded so that there is no fear of the adjustment slipping back. Turn the foot brake wing nut (on the offside of the brake cross shaft) in the same direction until there is only 2 in. or thereabouts of free movement on the pedal.

If the wing nuts are found to be too stiff to be moved by the fingers, penetrating oil and a suitable spanner will overcome the difficulty.

To check that the adjustments described have not been taken too far, raise the car up on all four wheels with the jack and suitable blocks and turn each wheel by hand with the hand brake off. They should all revolve freely, of course, and the adjustment should be slackened off if there is any tendency for the brakes to rub. An easier and more common method of testing the brakes is to drive the car a little way, stop without using the brakes, and then feel the drums. Any heat due to rubbing, will indicate that the adjustment is too close and requires slackening off. The 1937 cars have Girling adjusters for each of the four brakes, providing separate and independent adjustment and avoiding the necessity of jacking the car up. Each adjuster is screwed up until a resistance is felt and then slacked off one full quarter turn, indicated by a click. Each brake thus has the same clearance between the shoes and the drum.

The carburettor setting will not require altering unless exceptional circumstances require it. After the car has been run-in it may be found that the slow running of the engine can do with improvement. Before attempting this be sure and warm up the engine first and make the adjustments with the engine ticking over.

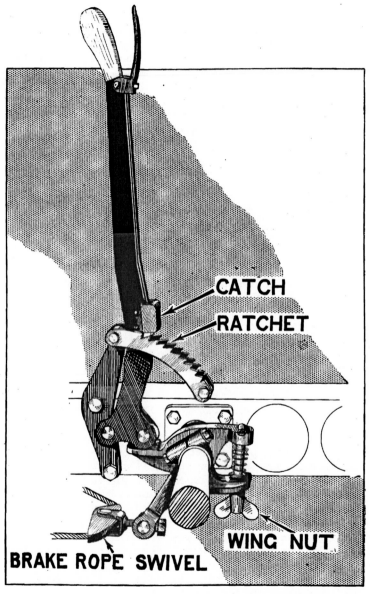

FIG. 25. HAND BRAKE ADJUSTMENT (EARLIER MODELS)

By turning the carburettor slow-running air regulator screw a new setting will be given. Usually a weaker mixture is required, provided by a slight turn in an anti-clockwise direction. A richer mixture is given if the screw is turned a little in the opposite direction.

Even slow running with responsive acceleration should be aimed at. If the air regulator screw is turned in the rich mixture direction (clockwise) as far as possible without rendering the slow running uneven the acceleration will be improved. If economy is of more importance, weaken the slow running mixture by turning the regulating screw in the anti-clockwise direction.

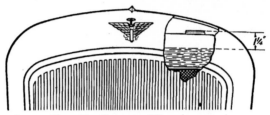

FIG. 26. CORRECT WATER-LEVEL

Actually it will be found that the amount of adjustment permissible without affecting the even slow running described is small. A too rich mixture will give uneven lumpy running known as "hunting," conversely a weak slow running mixture can be diagnosed by a tendency for the engine to stop at infrequent intervals or upon deceleration. At the same time as the air screw is adjusted the throttle stop screw should receive attention. As its title implies this screw determines the minimum throttle opening. To increase the slow running engine speed the minimum throttle opening can be increased by turning the stop screw in a clockwise direction. Conversely, the engine speed is decreased by turning the screw in the reverse direction.

The sparking plug points should be set to the gauge supplied in the tool kit, every time the engine is decarbonized, and the battery needs topping up regularly with distilled water. Each of the three cells has a porcelain plug which when removed should be carefully put on one side together with their respective rubber washers. The acid level can be seen through the plug holes and distilled water can be easily poured in until the level is just up to the top of the plate separators. The electrolyte gases freely when overcharged and frequent topping-up will be needed if the dynamo is allowed to supply more current than the battery requires. Warning—do not examine the battery electrolyte level with the aid of a naked flame. The gas given off—hydrogen—combines with the air to form an explosive mixture.

After topping-up all three cells replace the porcelain plugs with their rubber washers, clean the terminals, if at all corroded, and smother them well with vaseline.

The top of the distributor cover, the coil and the sparking plug insulation should be regularly cleaned. The moulded nuts securing the ignition leads in the distributor cover and the coil should be tested for tightness as a poor lead contact may result from a loose nut. The distributor contacts must be kept clean, so remove the distributor cover by releasing its two securing spring clips. Clean the interior of the distributor cover of any dust with a wiper and rub the four electrodes with a petrol rag. The central carbon brush must also be clean and free in its guide.

The contact breaker points are the most important from the cleanliness point of view. If the contacts look burnt they should be cleaned with a slip of very fine emery cloth and then rubbed over with the petrol rag. Check the gap with the gauge (which is combined with the small ignition screwdriver), when the contacts are fully open. If the gauge indicates a too large gap slacken the two screws in the contact plate with the ignition screwdriver, and move the plate until the gap is set to the thickness of the gauge.

Make certain, when retightening the two securing screws, that the adjustment is not disturbed when doing this.

Tyre wear is directly affected by neglect or failing to give attention to the correct tyre pressure. The recommended pressures are 22 lb. per sq. in. for the front tyres and 22 lb. for the rear, or 26 lb. for the rear if the car is fully laden. These figures should be strictly adhered to, and checked at frequent intervals using a tyre pressure gauge.

The cooling system requires hardly any attention from the owner beyond occasionally topping-up the level to replace any water lost by leakage or evaporation (see Fig. 26).

If the attentions just described are periodically applied to your Austin Seven a long life to all the working parts will be assured, and you will find your car will always give you a sweet and sure performance.

CHAPTER IV

The Recommended Lubricants. It is important to use only high quality lubricants. In addition to recommending the most suitable brands, in the following list the correct grades are given.

Standard Engine. Summer, Mobiloil "BB," Patent Castrol XL, "Triple" Shell, Essolube 50, Motorine C or Duckham's Aero N.P.3. Winter, Mobiloil "A," Patent Castrol "AA," Double Shell, Essolube 40, Motorine M or Duckham's Aero N.P.3.

Sports Engines (Summer): Mobiloil "D," Aero Shell, Patent Castrol XXL, Essolube Racer, Motorine B de Luxe or Duckham's Aero N.P.3.

(Winter): Mobiloil "BB," Double Shell, Patent Castrol XL, Essolube 50, Motorine C de Luxe or Duckham's Aero N.P.2.

Gear Box (Standard). Mobiloil "BB," Triple Shell, Patent Castrol XL, Essolube 50, Motorine C or Duckham's Aero N.P.3.

Sports Model. Mobiloil "D," Aero Shell, Patent Castrol XXL, Essolube Racer, Motorine B de Luxe or Duckham's Aero N.P.3.

Rear Axle and Steering Box. Mobiloil "C," Shell Spirax, Castrol D, Essoleum Expee, 110, Duckham's XS Press.

Wheels, Hubs and Grease Gun. Mobilgrease No. 4, Shell R.B. Grease, Castrolease Heavy, Esso Grease, Belmoline C or Duckham's HBB Grease.

Ignition Distributor Dynamo and Hand Oil Can. Gargoyle Velocite Oil D, Single Shell, Wakefield Oilit, Essolube 30, Price's Cycle Lubricating Oil or Duckham's Aero N.P.O.

Springs, Squeaks and Rusty Parts. Voco Penetrating Oil, Shell Penetrating Oil, Castrol Penetrating Oil, Essolube 30, Price's Penetrating Oil or Duckham's Easing Oil.

Upper Cylinder Lubrication. Gargoyle Upper Cylinder Lubricant, Shell Upper Cylinder Lubricant, Wakefield Castrollo, Petmix, Motorine U.C.L., or Duckham's Tablets.

ENGINE LUBRICATION SYSTEM

The life of a car as a whole depends essentially on its adequate lubrication. Fortunately Austin Seven owners find that their "Baby" is as simple in its lubrication requirements as it is easy to control.

The most important part of the car in this respect is obviously the prime mover—the engine. The high temperatures and pressures involved in the functioning of an engine necessitate adequate lubrication of the working parts by a suitably blended oil.

The Austin Seven engine has a special lubrication system, invented and patented by Sir Herbert Austin. This system has been employed in the design of the Austin Seven since the first of the present series was built in 1922. It is simple and depend-

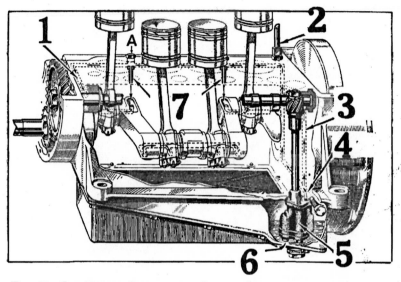

FIG. 27. THE ENGINE LUBRICATION SYSTEM (TWO-BEARING CRANKSHAFT)

1 = Oil passage to front camshaft bearing	4 = Delivery passage
2 = Connection to oil gauge	5 = Patent vane pump
3 = Oil passage to rear camshaft bearing	6 = Pump oil inlet
	7 = Oil jets
	A = Jet plug

able, incorporating a vane pump which pumps the oil along the oilways shown in Fig. 27.

The pressure of the oil in the system is quite low and rarely exceeds 5 lb. to the square inch. This pressure is sufficient to maintain a flow of oil from the sump to the jets in the top of the aluminium crankcase. The stream of oil from the jets impinges on the pockets in the crankshaft webs as they rotate, passes through suitably positioned oilways, and effectively lubricates the connecting rod big-ends. The camshaft bearings are lubricated from the same pump, and the oil spray flung from the revolving crankshaft and the oil mist present in the crankcase, lubricates the crankshaft roller bearings, the connecting rod little ends, the pistons and the cylinder walls. Lubrication of the valve stems is provided for by breathers in the valve chest at the rear of the valve cover. The oil in its circulation then drips down the inside of the crankcase on to the gauze filter above the sump cover. The strainer filters the oil from dirt, road grit and other impurities which the mesh will not pass.

Fig. 28. Using Dipstick to Ascertain Oil Level in Crankcase

The vane pump circulates the oil after it has passed the strainer, thus ensuring that the least amount of foreign matter present in the oil is not passed on to the bearings.

The 1937 series employs plain, pressure-fed centre bearings for the crankshaft and camshaft.

The conscientious Seven owner will make a habit of regularly inspecting the level of the oil in the crankcase of his engine by using the dipstick provided for the purpose (Fig. 28). This examination should be made about once a week or more often, according to the amount of use given to the car.

Oil should be added through the oil filler tube to bring the level up to the "FULL" mark on the dipstick again, if it is found to have fallen below. It is as well, particularly with a new car, to make this a regular practice. A new engine, although it may use little oil for the first two or three thousand miles, will be developing much higher temperatures at its working surfaces than later on when it is well run-in. Thus the lubrication requirements of a new engine are of supreme importance. It must be ensured, when testing the level, that the engine is stopped and the car on level ground, if a true indication is to be obtained. It may be found necessary to dip, wipe and replace the dipstick more than once before a satisfactory reading is given.. If the engine has been stopped for some time, say overnight, a more exact indication, providing the car is level, will be given by the dipstick, as all the oil will have drained down from the higher parts of the crankcase into the sump.

When actually replenishing, always use fresh oil of the correct blend and grade as detailed at the commencement of this chapter. These oils are, by the way, stamped on the oil filler tube cap by the manufacturer, so that the owner will have the necessary information in front of him when he comes to replenish his crankcase, even if he has forgotten the names of the brands and has not his Handbook with him.

While it is quite safe to run the engine for a long time with the oil level below the full mark, there is the ever-present danger of always leaving this duty until some more convenient time, until eventually through lack of oil the engine seizes up, involving a heavy repair bill. A quarter of an inch above the bottom of the dipstick is the lowest level to which the oil should be allowed to fall as a low level involves the risk of partial or complete failure of the system. The motion of the moving car often causes the pump to be starved by surging when only a small quantity of oil is in the sump. Therefore, always make a habit of looking at your dipstick before undertaking a long journey, and top-up to the correct level with fresh oil if necessary.

It will be noticed at the beginning of the chapter that an alternative engine and gearbox oil is available for summer and winter use. Temperature has an important influence on the viscosity of oils. In hot weather oil is more "runny" and will pour more easily than it will in winter, when it is often quite treacly. It can readily be understood then, that by using a thinner oil in cold weather, as provided for in the list of recommended lubricants, much easier starting will be obtained, with lower friction losses, than if the more viscous oil used during the summer is retained. It is surprising what a difference there is between cold oil at ordinary air temperature and the same oil at its normal working sump temperature. The latter is nearly always ten to twelve times less viscous than the former, while at the crankshaft bearings of a hot engine the oil may be quite forty times thinner than when cold. Owners will readily understand, therefore, how necessary it is to warm up the engine before draining the crankcase oil if this is to be quickly and thoroughly performed.

An even more important aspect of this preliminary running of the engine before draining is that the oil, besides being hot, will be thoroughly agitated and will then carry away most of the impurities that necessitates the change.

The termination of the first 500 miles should mean the first change of oil for the engine. During this time it can be assumed that the car has been lightly driven and as all the parts are new and unworn very little oil should have been required to maintain the level.

In spite of the fact that all the component parts of a new engine are skilfully manufactured to close limits by machine tools, leaving the working surfaces with a glass-like finish, it is yet a rough engine in the proper sense of the word when it is compared with a similar engine that has been run-in with its parts burnished and bedded down by its functioning. The high spots of the new parts have to be actually rubbed down, and until they are polished away they are subjected to high pressures and temperatures. The end of the first 500 miles should see the best part of the running-in process achieved, but the oil has had a bad time from the heat in the process and it will contain a considerable amount of metal that has been burnished from the moving parts. The metal particles are not the only foreign matter present as gradual contamination has taken place to deprive the oil of its value as a lubricant. Starting the engine up from cold with the strangler in action too long, and prolonged periods of idling are responsible for the presence of unused petrol in the oil. The petrol has passed the pistons, washed the cylinder walls of their protective oil film and remains to dilute the crankcase oil. This petrol, and also condensed water from the exhaust gases that has also passed the pistons (look at the inside of your oil filler cap the next time you remove it and notice the beads of moisture), do not so seriously affect the lubricant as at first glance it may appear. Re-evaporation by engine heat and the breathing of the crankcase ensures that only a small percentage of this petrol and water remains. Other diluents of the lubricant from the products of combustion besides the water already mentioned, are mostly acids. Therefore, it will readily be understood that the oil must be changed for fresh, and as has been shown, most of the impurities will be run clear if arrangements are made for the draining to be done after the car has come in from a run so that, being hot and agitated, the oil will carry with it most of the sludge that may be present in the system.

To drain the engine sump the drain plug underneath the engine at the rear must be unscrewed and removed after a suitable receptacle has been placed below to catch the waste oil. Jacking up the front of the car or placing it on a slight slope will facilitate the process of draining and render it less easy for sludge to adhere to the bottom of the sump cover.

When the last drops have indicated that the draining is complete, replace the drain plug with its fibre washer and insert a light flushing oil, which can be bought for the purpose, into the crankcase through the oil filler tube. Remove the sparking plugs so that the engine can be rotated easily, and turn the starting handle until satisfied that the inside of the engine has been thoroughly flushed out. Then unscrew the sump plug again and let the flushing oil drain away. It is unwise to use petrol or paraffin in place of a genuine flushing oil, as a proportion will inevitably be left in the oilways and the interior of the crankcase to dilute to a considerable extent the new oil when it is poured into the engine.

Carefully clean the drain plug and its fibre washer when replacing them once more and also the seating round the plug orifice, as it is important to ensure that no grit or other matter will prevent a good seal being made when the drain plug is tightened home or oil drips will subsequently prove themselves a nuisance on the garage floor.

With the drain plug and washer carefully replaced approximately half a gallon of one of the approved brands of oil can now be poured into the engine through the oil filler tube.

Owners of the Austin Seven sports models will find that they will require a gallon as these cars have a double capacity sump.

The engine is now ready for a further spell of work, and the oil need not be changed again until the next 2,000 miles have been recorded on the speedometer.

Before starting up, however, it is as well to rotate the engine by hand so that the fresh oil is distributed by the pump along the oil passages.

At the next change of oil and subsequently at every other change, or every 4,000 miles, the sump cover or oil reservoir ought to be removed and the interior of the crankcase thoroughly cleaned (Fig. 29). Fourteen setscrews secure the reservoir to the crankcase and each has a plain oval and a spring washer which must be carefully replaced when the reservoir is refitted. After the reservoir has been removed a further ten setscrews will have to be undone to release the gauze oil tray now disclosed.

This strainer is easily cleaned by swilling in either paraffin or petrol and by using a brush to clean the gauze. Be careful to use a brush that does not shed its bristles and refrain from using fluffy rags. A portion of a bristle or a piece of fluff may easily lead to an oil stoppage if allowed to be pumped along the system,

FIG. 29. CLEANING INTERIOR OF SUMP COVER

so see that no strands or pieces of cleaning material are left after the interior of the crankcase has been thoroughly cleaned.

A good oil-tight joint must be made of the bottom cover and a new joint washer is usually desirable when replacing the strainer and cover. Clean carefully both the joint surfaces in the crankcase and on the cover, and smear the washer with grease on both sides. After securing the gauze strainer by its ten retaining setscrews (Fig. 30) place the greased washer on the rim of the bottom cover (Fig. 31) and offer it up to the crankcase. The retaining setscrews of both the gauze tray and the sump cover should first be tightened finger tight all round, after it has been ensured that all the setscrews have their proper washers. They should then be tightened up a little at a time all round, so that an even pressure is obtained over the entire joint surface. If this is done, and a box spanner used to tighten the screws a few degrees at a time, a good joint will result.

It is a good plan, when finally tightening the screws, to start at the centre of the gauze strainer or the cover, and work outwards to the ends until the screws are all dead tight (see Fig. 32).

The method of lubricating the crankshaft webs has already

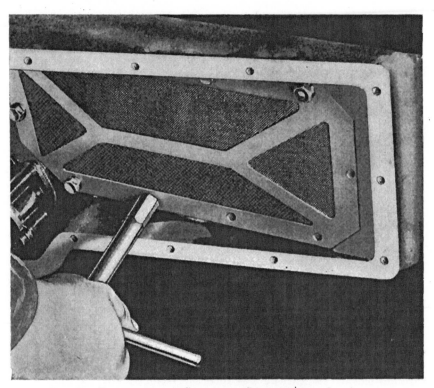

FIG. 30. REPLACING THE SETSCREWS SECURING THE OIL STRAINER TO THE INTERIOR OF THE CRANKCASE

been explained, but the jets through which the oil is forced down into the pockets of the rotating webs will benefit with an occasional clean. This is best done by removing the covering plugs (Fig. 33) at the top of the crankcase and poking a piece of wire, not bigger in diameter than $\frac{1}{16}$ in., through the jets. While doing this it is as well to remember that any dirt poked out of the jets by this method will fall into the crankshaft pockets if the crankshaft is allowed to lie in its normal position. Therefore, before cleaning the jets, turn the starting handle until it is on compression with the crankshaft throws in a vertical position and thus out of the way.

Before leaving the subject of engine lubrication, the special oiling system adopted for the Sports model must be dealt with. The crankshaft bearings (Fig. 34) are lubricated by splash but the connecting rod big ends and the camshaft are fed

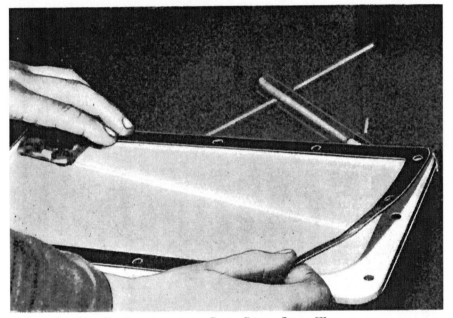

FIG. 31. REPLACING THE SUMP COVER JOINT WASHER

under full pressure. The oil is forced from the pump into chamber *B* in the crankcase front cover. From this chamber the oil passes through the bored starting dog into the front end of the hollow crankshaft and is then distributed to the four connecting rod bearings.

The normal pressure of the oil is high, being about 50 lb. per sq. in. under normal working conditions. The oil is prevented from escaping from the front end of chamber *B* by a leather washer *A*, between a facing on the crankcase front and a flange on the starting handle shaft, the joint being rendered oil-tight by the pressure of the oil itself. Should a leakage of oil occur at this point, the cover must be removed and a new washer fitted.

TRANSMISSION AND CHASSIS LUBRICATION

The importance of attending to the lubrication of the transmission and chassis in a systematic manner cannot be emphasized too strongly. It is the little-and-often that does the trick

and enables the car to give of its best. It is not fair to leave the
steering connections, for instance, without lubricant for thousands
of miles, during which time water and road dust, an excellent
abrasive mixture, have been wearing down the working surfaces,

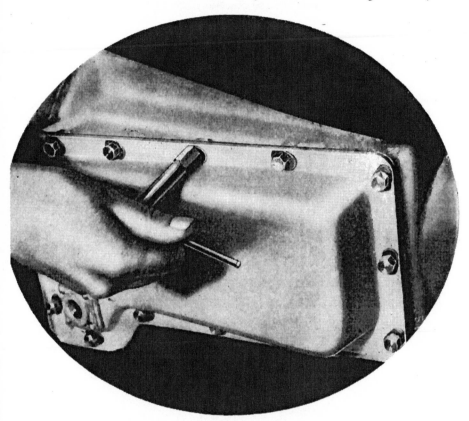

Fig. 32. Refitting the Sump Cover Securing Setscrews

and then afterwards expect to put matters right by flooding the
parts concerned with lubricant.

It will be found that, given a little thought, the necessary oiling
and greasing jobs can be rapidly disposed of if a regular scheme is
formulated and pursued.

To check the level of the oil in the gearbox first run the car
on to level ground, then take out the front floor mats and remove
the small plate revealed.

Then unscrew the oil level plug to be seen on the nearside of
the gearbox and inspect the level (see Fig. 35). The oil should

just reach the bottom of the thread and fresh engine oil should be poured in if the level is below. Then replace the screwed plug, the small cover and the front mats. This attention should be observed about every 200 miles.

The same oils recommended for the engine are suitable for use

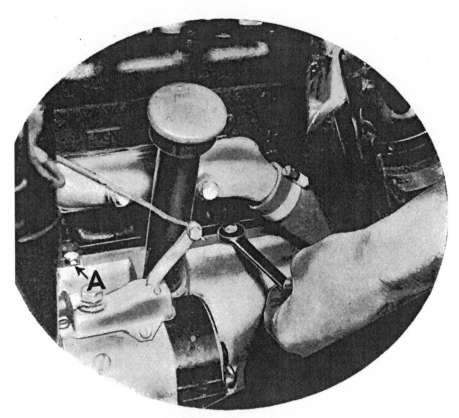

FIG. 33. REMOVING THE PLUGS *A* TO ALLOW THE OIL JETS TO BE CLEANED

in the gearbox (see page 40). This ensures a light, easy gear change.

The running-in process, as it affects the gearbox, results in the contamination of the gearbox oil with minute metal particles abraded from the interior working surfaces, and it thus requires to be changed quite early, at about 1,000 miles.

A pint and a half of fresh oil of a recommended brand must be poured into the gearbox after the old has been drained away.

The drain plug at the bottom of the gearbox which has first to be removed can be readily reached from underneath the car.

The plate covering the clutch pit drain hole will be dismounted when the drain plug, that incidentally secures it, is unscrewed.

The importance of ensuring that lubricant is warmed up before draining was explained when dealing with the engine (page 43). It will be taken for granted, then, that the car has had a run sufficient to warm the gearbox oil and ensure its thorough draining when the drain plug is removed.

The old oil will then drain out quickly, and having been recently

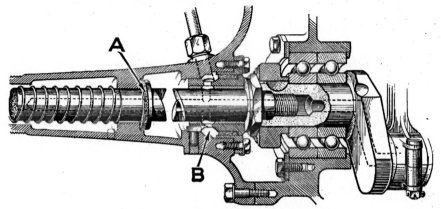

FIG. 34. THE FRONT END OF THE SPORTS
CRANKSHAFT

agitated by the functioning of the gearbox, will carry most of the impurities with it.

After allowing the last drops of the old oil to drip into a suitable receptacle, carefully clean the drain plug and its fibre washer and the joint face on the gearbox. Then refit the drain plug and washer, not forgetting the clutch pit drain hole cover, and screw up tight. Remove the combined level and filler plug, if this has not already been done, and fill up with the pint and a half of new oil which is in readiness. This should give an oil level up to the bottom of the thread in the plug hole.

After this first change the oil need not be renewed again until a further 5,000 miles has been undergone, but the level must be maintained over this period by regular inspection and topping-up.

The clutch requires weekly attention in the form of a few drops of engine oil through the oiler tube (*F*, Fig. 35). This is rendered accessible upon removing the rubber gearbox cover or the toe plate which is in front of the gearbox.

FIG. 35. EXAMINING THE GEARBOX OIL LEVEL

F is the clutch lubricator

The oil in the back axle should be changed at the same time as the gearbox is dealt with, namely, at the termination of the first thousand miles. Whereas engine oil is suitable for use in the gearbox a special lubricant is required for the back axle. The brands recommended are given on page 40, and a quick-action attachment is provided with the grease gun to enable this lubricant

Fig. 36. Injecting a Charge of Lubricant into the Back
Axle with the Quick-action End of the Grease Gun

to be rapidly injected into the back axle (Fig. 36) either when
topping-up or refilling. As with the gearbox there is a combined
oil filler and level plug at the rear of the back axle case. Oil
should be added if upon inspection the level is not up to the oil
level orifice. This inspection should be made at intervals of about
200 miles.

To change the oil remove the drain plug from the base of the
back axle and let the old oil flow into a can shallow enough to

pass under the axle. Replace the drain plug and fibre washer when the axle is empty and inject back axle oil of one of the recommended brands until it flows out of the level orifice when the grease gun is removed.

To use the quick-action attachment of the grease gun take out the cork plug and chain and fill with the special lubricant. Screw the cover over the grease ram and fit the quick-action nozzle in place of the cap at the other end. When the gun is now used with the quick-action end at the orifice, a large quantity of lubricant will be rapidly injected.

If too much oil has been injected through over-zealous use of the gun, do not replace the filler plug until the surplus oil has drained out again and the level is correct, i.e. up to the mouth of the level orifice. Then carefully clean the plug and its fibre washer and tighten home. It is important to ensure that all excess oil is allowed to escape by this means as if it is retained within the axle case it will not benefit the mechanism in any way, and the probability is that a proportion will work past the oil seals on the axle shafts and reach the brakes to impair their efficiency.

If an exact measure of the back axle contents is required to ensure that the axle is not over-filled, ⅞ pint will bring the oil up to the right level.

The next 5,000 miles will require this oil to be changed again, and during the intervening period of the car's running regular inspection and topping-up will be necessary at about every 2,000 miles.

Continuing with the transmission the new needle-bearing type universal joints do not require lubrication except at the front splined end of the propeller shaft which requires attention once a month at the grease nipple provided, using the ordinary grease in the grease gun.

The same grease is also required weekly at the torque tube (Fig. 37). This is accessible through the small cover on the transmission tunnel inside the car. The steering connections are important and the grease nipples should be wiped clean to make sure that no road grit, dust, etc., is forced into the bearings with the fresh grease.

When applying the grease gun to these parts continue until the new grease has forced out all the old, which should then be removed with a rag.

It is advisable when greasing the steering swivels to jack up each front wheel in turn to take the weight of the car and thus ensure that the fresh grease will penetrate to all the working surfaces.

There are five points requiring attention by the grease-gun and three where the oil-can is needed. The steering cross-tube

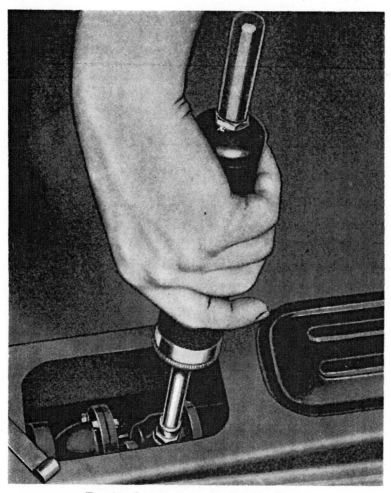

FIG. 37. LUBRICATING THE TORQUE TUBE

(Fig. 38) has a grease nipple at each end which can be easily got at, although the car may have to be moved a little to give sufficient room between the wheel spokes to operate the gun.

The same grade of oil used for the back axle is also used for the steering gearbox. A charge once a month is required by grease gun through the nipple on the gearbox casing. The nipple can be reached quite easily from the front of the scuttle.

warning is necessary here—don't inject an excessive quantity of lubricant—here again it is a case of a-little-and-often. All

FIG. 38. GREASING THE STEERING CROSS-TUBE

surplus grease will gradually accumulate up the steering column until eventually it may exude at the top, under the steering wheel, to the probable detriment to either driver or passenger's clothing. Oil should occasionally be applied to the hole lubricating the steering column bearing under the wheel.

A weekly dose of oil from the oil-can will serve for the ends of the steering side-tube where the ball pins work in their sockets. The brake-cam spindles that actuate the brake shoes, are automatically lubricated, those at the rear having self-lubricating

bushes, while those at the front receive supplies of lubricant from
the swivel-pin greasers (see *B*, Fig. 58). These bearings, therefore, and also the rest of the brake mechanism, need not concern
the owner except for a few drops of oil occasionally applied to
the working parts of the system.

An important, albeit only an occasional job, is to apply a little
oil to the ball flange and cups that form the anchorage for the

FIG. 39. SHOWING HOW WHEEL HUBS ARE LUBRICATED

A is plug to be removed to allow old grease to escape as fresh is inserted
by screwing up hub cap. . *B*, *C*, *D*, and *E* are steering and spring shackle
greasing points

radius rods. This point of anchorage is at the centre of the cross
member just below the rear of the gearbox.

To lubricate the wheel hubs (Fig. 39), jack up each in turn
and remove the wheel to give access to the hub. The wheels on
the Austin Seven are easily removed by slackening the retaining
nuts a few turns, pulling the wheel away and giving it a sharp
turn in an anti-clockwise direction. This will bring the large
holes in the wheel centre over the nuts and the wheel can then
be pulled straight off.

Gargoyle Grease B, a special waterproof grease that does not
easily leak past the oil seals, is the recommended grease for Austin
Seven hubs. It should be applied to the hubs through the nipples
or plugs provided. If it is desired, the front hub caps can be
removed, filled with grease and screwed in place again. If the

FIG. 40. GREASING THE REAR SPRING ANCHORAGE

plug is taken out of the hub casing the orifice will allow the grease to enter easily and air or old grease to escape. This is the more usual procedure adopted by owners as it is then not necessary to empty the grease gun of its contents, refill with the special hub grease and then afterwards have the trouble of charging the grease gun again with its more usual everyday grease.

The front spring shackles and the spring anchorages on the rear axle (Fig. 40) together have six grease nipples that require a charge from the grease gun once a week. Old oil drained from the engine or gearbox will do to brush the springs with. If this is done occasionally the springs will not rust and squeak but will maintain their resilience, and the comfort of the users of the car will be assured. Patent Castrol penetrating oil or Voco penetrating oil (see also list on page 40), both light oils that creep

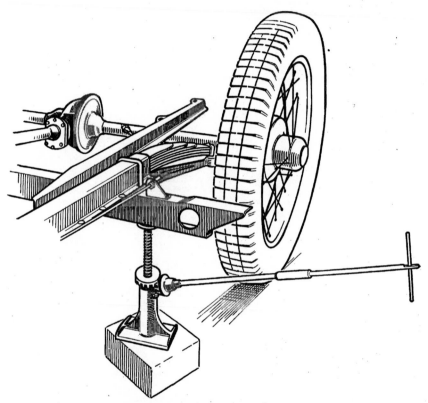

FIG. 41. THE CHASSIS SHOULD BE LIFTED AS SHOWN TO ALLOW OIL TO BE FORCED BETWEEN THE SPRING LEAVES FOR EASY RIDING

easily, will also serve this purpose excellently and will quickly penetrate between the spring leaves (Fig. 41).

The spring leaves are made slightly hollow, and when they are finally assembled and clipped together a thin reservoir or film of oil is easily maintained between the leaves. The action of the springs tends to spread the oil and ensures a smooth flexible suspension.

Lastly, when dealing with any of the oiling and greasing jobs first see to it that the oil can, grease gun and the nipples, etc., are

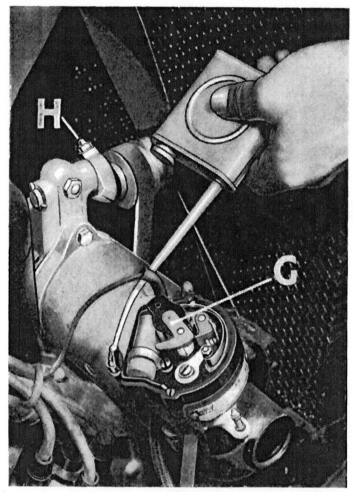

FIG. 42. THE ELECTRIC UNITS SHOULD BE SPARINGLY
LUBRICATED; A FEW DROPS ONLY ARE REQUIRED

G is the distributor rotor; *H* is the fan spindle greaser

clean. If a nipple will not pass its charge of grease, remove it and
fit a new one if it is still obstinate after cleaning with petrol.

As is well known, electrical equipment will not suffer a super-
fluity of lubricant (Fig. 42). A little oil in the wrong place may
prove to be a source of trouble later on. The electric windscreen
wiper, the dynamo and the electric starter, all have their lubrication requirements provided for when they are manufactured

and no subsequent attention in this direction will be required from the owner. A lubricator is fitted to the distributor spindle bearing and a drop or two of oil will be required here about every month or every 1,000 miles, whichever comes first. If the distributor cap is removed a smear of vaseline can be given to the distributor cam, and an occasional drop of oil to the top of the distributor spindle to lubricate the automatic advance and retard mechanism, and a very occasional drop on the contact breaker pivot.

To get at the top of the distributor spindle the rotor will have to be pulled off but the screw then rendered visible must not be unscrewed. The oil will penetrate round it and reach the automatic mechanism below. Make sure that the rotor is replaced accurately in the same position as before, as it will only fit properly in the one position.

The body does not possess many moving parts but a little oil or grease at regular intervals at such places as the door locks and hinges, windscreen hinges and securing catch, and direction indicator pivots, will go a long way to ensure the easy operation of the various moving components of the body and prevent elusive squeaks arising later on.

CHAPTER V

THE busy Austin Seven owner often has little spare time in which to attend to the many diverse requirements of his car.

By the same token he often has little time with which to assimilate the necessary information contained in the manufacturer's literature.

An easy solution for this type of owner, is, of course, for him to take advantage of the excellent flat-rate servicing facilities provided by the hundreds of Austin Dealers up and down the country.

For the owner who wishes, however, to maintain his car in good condition himself, the following Summary of Regular Attentions has been drawn up.

By its guidance, all the greasing and oiling jobs, etc., can be done regularly and systematically, and will prevent any important attention being overlooked through the owner's too hasty perusal of the literature appertaining to his car.

The summary is based on the assumption that the maximum weekly mileage does not exceed 300.

REGULAR ATTENTIONS

Every Day. Examine water level in radiator and fill up to within 1¼ in. of the filler cap.

Examine oil level in the crankcase by the dipstick and add more fresh oil if necessary.

Fill up with petrol if necessary. The tank holds 5 gallons.

Every Week. With the grease gun charge the four front spring shackle pins. The two rear spring pins. The two front axle swivel pins. Each end of the steering cross tube. The front end of the torque tube.

Oil both steering side-tube joints.

Examine the brakes, and adjust if necessary.

Test the tyres for correct pressure and examine them for cuts.

Every Month. Examine the gearbox oil level which should be up to the bottom of the plug hole. Contents 1½ pints.

Examine the back axle oil level which should be up to the bottom of the plug hole. Add fresh oil if necessary using the special adaptor on the grease gun. Contents ⅔ pint.

Grease all hubs.

Oil the clutch release ring.

Inject oil into the steering gearbox.

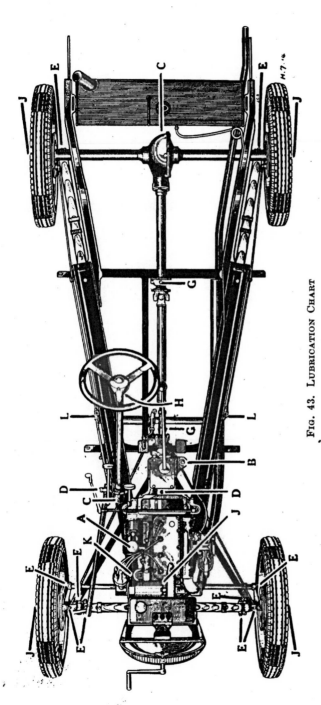

FIG. 43. LUBRICATION CHART

A. Crankcase, replenish to full mark on dip-stick *weekly*. B. Gearbox, replenish *monthly*. C. Rear axle and steering box, replenish *monthly*—Special oil. D. Clutch withdrawal sleeve and steering side tube, oil *weekly*. E. Cross tube (2), Swivel axles (2), Spring shackles (6), grease *weekly*. G. Torque tube, front end, propeller shaft, splined end, grease *monthly*. H. Top of steering column, oil *monthly*. K. Distributor, oil sparingly every 1000 miles. L. Brake and throttle control joints, and brake pedal shaft, oil *weekly*.

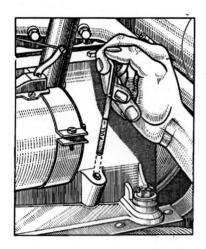

FIG. 44. EXAMINING OIL LEVEL
OF CRANKCASE

FIG. 46. COMBINED GEARBOX
OIL LEVEL AND FILLER PLUG

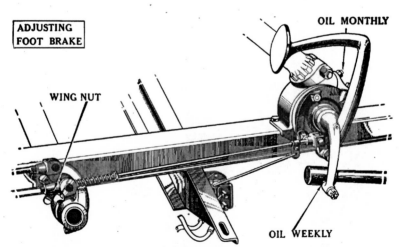

FIG. 45. STEERING LUBRICATION POINTS AND FOOT BRAKE
ADJUSTMENT

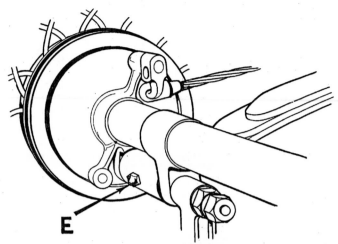

FIG. 47. REAR BRAKE ROPE CONNECTION AND SPRING
ANCHORAGE GREASE NIPPLE

Oil the braking system and all control joints.

Examine the battery, top-up with distilled water if necessary.

Give ignition distributor oiler a few drops of light oil.

Grease the fan spindle.

Every Two Months. Change engine oil.

Clean and set gap of sparking plugs.

Every Four Months. Dismount engine sump, clean gauze strainer and interior of engine.

Change gearbox oil.

Change back axle oil.

OCCASIONAL ATTENTIONS

Examine all nuts and bolts such as road spring clips, cylinder head nuts, wheel nuts. Examine steering connections, the radius rod anchorage below the gearbox, and the torque tube socket.

FIG. 48. CLEANING CRANKCASE
OIL JETS WITH THIN WIRE

Clean the float chamber strainers and the petrol filter, the oil reservoir gauze (when the engine oil is changed) and also ensure that the oil jets in the crankcase (Fig. 48) are clean. Drain the gearbox and the back axle and refill with fresh oil.

Flush the radiator through. Clean the ignition distributor and the coil and clean and adjust the contact breaker points and also the dynamo and starter commutators. Adjust the tappets, and the fan belt, decarbonize the engine and grind-in the valves. Check the alinement of the front wheels.

The top of the distributor cover and the sparking plug insulator should be regularly cleaned. The moulded nuts securing the high tension leads in the distributor cover and the coil should be tested for tightness as a poor lead contact may result from a loose nut. The distributor contacts must be kept clean, so remove the distributor cover by releasing its two securing spring clips. Clean the interior of the distributor cover of any dust with a wiper and rub the four electrodes with a petrol rag. The central carbon brush must also be clean and free in its guide.

The contact breaker points are the most important from the cleanliness point of view. If the contacts look burnt they should be cleaned with a slip of very fine emery cloth and then rubbed over with the petrol rag. Check the gap with the gauge which is combined with the ignition screwdriver, when the contacts are fully open. If the gauge indicates too large a gap slacken the two screws in the contact plate with the ignition screwdriver and move the plate until the correct setting is obtained ; afterwards resecure the two screws.

CHAPTER VI

MAINTENANCE AND OVERHAULING

THE maintenance of a reliable small car like the Austin Seven does not take much of the owner's time, and the instructions in this chapter will enable him to give his car the necessary attention that every car requires.

The regular examination of all bolts and nuts, such as road spring clips, wheel nuts, cylinder head nuts, especially when the car is new, is important. So also is the inspection of parts, such as the radius rod anchorage below the gearbox, the torque tube socket, and the steering connections, as has been emphasized in the "Summary of Regular Attentions," Chapter V.

DECARBONIZING

Decarbonizing and grinding-in the valves are both jobs performed by owners. They are, at the same time, jobs that can be confidently and successfully undertaken by anyone with only a slight mechanical knowledge.

The Austin Seven, with its side-valve engine with detachable head, is renowned for the simplicity of its design and its all-round accessibility, fundamentals that make servicing operations so easy for the owner driver, and allow him to enjoy "looking after" his car. So simple is the job of decarbonizing that it is only necessary to remove the sparking-plug leads and the water outlet connection (one setscrew, after draining off the cooling water) before actually removing the cylinder head, also for decarbonizing or grinding-in the valves no special tools have to be bought. The contents of the tool kit meet all the requirements of either of these jobs.

Decarbonizing need not necessarily involve grinding-in the valves, although the same dismantling and reassembling of the engine have made these two maintenance items almost synonymous. If the compression of the cylinders when tested with the starting handle is up to standard, and equal for all four cylinders, decarbonizing can be effected without disturbing the valves.

The need for decarbonizing is usually made evident to the owner by a metallic knocking sound coming from the engine when it is pulling hard, especially at low engine speeds.

This knocking noise is due to the excess of carbon deposited on the surfaces of the combustion spaces and on the tops of the pistons, causing irregular and local areas of combustion with the

67

incidental rapid increase in pressure giving rise to the knocking sounds. Combustion should be as even as possible, starting from the sparking plug points and spreading through the charge, giving a not too-rapid explosion. The piston will then receive a comparatively steady sustained pressure instead of the sharp violent one.

Excess of carbon in an engine is also responsible for irregular running by its becoming incandescent from the heat of combustion and then firing the incoming charge prematurely.

Owners may have noticed also that this can happen with a hot, carbonized engine when the ignition is switched off; the incandescent carbon firing the charges as they are inspired and enabling the engine to run for several further revolutions.

When an engine is in this state, the earliest opportunity should be taken to decarbonize it. If some time must necessarily elapse before the job can be undertaken the knocking noise from the engine can be temporarily alleviated by using an anti-knock fuel with an alcohol or tetra-ethyl content, or by retarding the ignition. The latter will, of course, normally impair the performance, but it will slow down the combustion rate slightly, and if the driver engages a lower gear earlier than usual, knocking will be rendered less obtrusive. The engine will not run so well in this state; the loss of efficiency due to the carbon is self-evident by the loss of power, overheating, and increased consumption of petrol.

A good indication as to the state of the combustion spaces as far as carbon is concerned can be obtained from the condition of the sparking plugs. If, on removal for examination, the plugs have acquired a considerable amount of carbon round the base of the electrodes, a similar state can be assumed to exist in the combustion chambers.

Before getting down to the actual job it will be as well to warm up the engine. It will be found to be much easier to break the joints and unscrew the cylinder head nuts, etc., if this is done.

Drain the water from the cooling system by turning the tap at the offside of the base of the radiator block. The capacity of the cooling system is roughly 9½ pints. Therefore, if the winter anti-freeze solution is to be retained, a receptacle large enough to contain this amount should be placed under the draining orifice. If, however, it is not desired to keep the cooling water, and a drain is handy, the best plan is to run the car near by and then run the water off.

Then disconnect the earth lead from the battery for safety's sake, and to give unrestricted access to the engine when working remove the bonnet. To do this release the single bonnet hinge fixing at the centre of the bonnet stay. The bonnet stay is the steel pressing, secured at scuttle and radiator, that lies underneath the bonnet hinge. With this fixing undone, one side of the bonnet should be raised and the bonnet completely removed from the opposite side, grasping the bonnet sides at front and rear and moving it slightly to the front of the car, so withdrawing the rear end of the bonnet hinge from its socket at the scuttle. Damage to the cellulosed wings and radiator cowl will be guarded against, if a friend is persuaded to lend a hand in manipulating the bonnet.

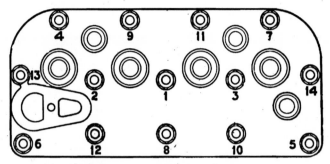

Fig. 49. The Correct Order of Undoing and Securing the Cylinder Head Nuts

With the bonnet clear, it may be thought that access to the engine will be increased if the horn is removed. If this is so, before removing the horn, first disconnect both horn wires.

The cooling system should be drained by now, so that the radiator can be separated from the cylinder head. To do this it is not necessary to break the water outlet hose joints, as the water outlet branch can be detached by unscrewing its single holding-down setscrew.

Under the branch will be found a rubber joint washer which must be carefully put aside for replacement when refitting the branch.

Remove the sparking plug leads, replace the plug terminals, and tuck the leads out of the way.

The cylinder head holding-down nuts (Fig. 49) can now be slackened all round before unscrewing them individually. This procedure is to prevent the cylinder head from being strained. There are fourteen of these nuts with metal washers underneath, and when these have been removed the sparking plugs can be unscrewed and the two special lifting screws provided in the tool kit screwed into the two outside plug holes.

By grasping the handles of these screws firmly and pulling up with a slight rocking motion the head will normally be withdrawn off its holding-down studs with little trouble. In the event of the head proving obstinate, however, one or two judicio us mallet blows may loosen it.

An alternative method of overcoming difficulty in removing the cylinder head is to refrain from unscrewing the sparking plugs until the head has been withdrawn. In which case, by rotating the crankshaft with the starting handle (with the ignition switched off, of course), after the holding-down nuts have been removed, it will be found that the compression of the engine will break the joint and free it enough to enable it to be drawn off the studs by hand.

When actually withdrawing the head, note carefully if the joint washer or gasket is stuck to the cylinder head or to the cylinder block, or if it is stuck to both. In the latter case, free it gently from either surface and then lift the cylinder head clear.

If the gasket has been left on the cylinder block it, too, will have to be carefully lifted off the monobloc studs. This is best done as near the horizontal as possible to avoid damaging its copper asbestos washer joint. If it sticks on one or more of the threaded studs it will have to be eased away carefully. When putting the gasket in a safe place, make a slight mark on the upper surface, for identification purposes, to ensure that it is replaced the same way up. Be careful not to make too definite a mark, or the efficiency of the washer may be impaired.

It sometimes happens that a cylinder head nut binds on its stud so that the stud itself is unscrewed from the cylinder block. To replace the stud firmly in the monobloc when the head is clear, screw the stud in its tapped hole, using a spanner on the nut that caused the trouble. When the stud has been firmly screwed down to the limit of its lower threaded length, the obstinate nut can be "started" by continuing to turn it in the right-handed direction. Once free on the stud it can be easily run off the thread, leaving the stud firm in the monobloc. If the nut has been loosened beforehand it will be necessary to use another nut to lock it before attempting to replace the stud.

The carbon on the cylinder head and on the tops of the pistons and round the heads of the valves can now be scraped off. If the sparking plugs have not been removed, remove them before attempting to clean the cylinder head and place them on one side for cleaning and adjusting. The condition of the carbon deposits in the engine indicate the mechanical condition of the engine generally. A hard, dry deposit shows that the oil consumption is good, and therefore the piston, piston rings, etc., are not unduly worn. The reverse is shown if the carbon is soft and oily.

Use a small scraper or a screwdriver for removing the carbon, but before doing so turn the crankshaft with the starting handle to bring two pistons to the top of their stroke. Stuff pieces of rag into the other open bores to prevent the intrusion of loosened carbon, and, although it is not strictly necessary, some owners may consider it worth while also to close the water openings in the cylinder block with rag. Take particular care, if this is done, to remove these same scraps of rag, taking a roll call if need be, for if one of those pieces slips down and is not recovered, it will ultimately obstruct the circulation system and cause overheating.

With the tools selected scrape all the carbon from off the tops of the two pistons (being careful not to scratch unduly the soft aluminium alloy) and the interior edges of their cylinder bores. The oil consumption will not be affected if care is taken not to remove the carbon from the chamfered edges of the pistons. Then clean the deposits from all the valve heads and the adjacent combustion surfaces, afterwards rubbing all the scraped areas with a paraffin or petrol rag. This will clear away all the loose carbon dust and reveal the patches missed by the scraper. After dealing with these and ensuring that all the carbon has been removed, the crankshaft can be given a half turn to bring the other pair of pistons to the top of their cylinders; they will push out the rags.

These can be shaken out, used to wipe the cylinder bores of the decarbonized pistons, shaken again, and stuffed into those cylinders while the other two pistons are dealt with.

Carefully scrape the carbon deposits from the piston crowns, and afterwards clean with paraffin rag as was done with the first pair of pistons.

This done, attention can be given to the cylinder head, and, turned upside down, it can be scraped free from carbon. The interior rounded surfaces will not be so easy to clean as the piston crowns, etc., but if a suitably rounded tool is used the job will not be unduly difficult. When all four combustion spaces in the cylinder head have been dealt with and cleaned out afterwards with the paraffin rag, clean the interior edges of the cylinder head gasket of carbon and examine it carefully for defects. If damaged replace it with a new gasket.

If it is not desired to grind in the valves, reassembly of the cylinder head and joint washer can be commenced.

Before doing so, see that all the parts are thoroughly clean, especially the contact surfaces—not a particle of carbon must be on one of them or an unsatisfactory joint may result. A good way to ensure that no carbon bits or dust will remain in the cylinder bores—especially round the chamfered edge of the piston crowns—is to squirt engine oil on the piston crowns and the cylinder walls and then rotate the crankshaft with the starting handle. It will be found that any carbon particles will be left on the cylinder walls by the receding pistons. It is then an easy matter alternately to wipe the surplus oil from the cylinder walls and turn the starting handle, until satisfied that all are clean.

If the gasket is a new one or if the old one is in good condition it should not be necessary to use gold size or any other sealing compound. If care has been taken to ensure that all the contacting surfaces are really clean, the gasket smeared with grease on both sides, and the head is pulled down evenly, a perfect joint will result. Before refitting the head make sure that no rags have been left in any of the cylinder bores or water ducts.

If the original gasket is used again see that the marked side is uppermost.

The gasket may stick on one or more of the holding-down studs; it is a flimsy affair and requires gentle handling. It had best be eased down the obstructing stud or studs with a suitable box spanner.

Replace the cylinder head and the oiled gasket and oil the cylinder head holding-down studs and nuts so that the nuts with their washers can be easily run down the threads by hand. When all the nuts are finger tight, tighten them further with a box spanner, giving each half a turn at a time in the order shown in Fig. 49, until all are tight home. The idea is to compress the whole surface of the gasket to get a good joint and also to prevent the head from being even slightly tipped at one end or a side, and so cause the casting to be strained.

With a good joint thus effected the sparking plugs can be replaced if they have been cleaned and have had their points set to the gauge supplied in the tool kit. The leads can then be replaced on the sparking plug terminals and the water outlet branch with its rubber washer replaced on the cylinder head. All that is left to be done is for the cooling system to be refilled with water or the original anti-freeze solution replaced—it being taken for granted, of course, that the drain tap has been closed.

Then, with assistance, replace the bonnet, and secure it to the bonnet support stay at its single fixing, and replace the battery negative lead after the horn and horn wires have been dealt with. The car is now ready for the road, but first warm up the engine and then run over the cylinder nuts with a box spanner. Tighten them again after the next 250 miles when the gasket, if it was a new one, will have settled down a little.

Grinding-in the Valves. Grinding-in the valves of the Austin Seven need not always be undertaken when the engine is decarbonized. It should suffice if the valves are ground-in about every other decarbonization, providing, of course, that the compression of the engine remains satisfactory in between times.

This can be tested with the starting handle, two complete turns of which will indicate the compression resistance of the four cylinders, and thus the condition of all eight valves. The compression resistance of the cylinders to the turning effort applied to the turning handle should be elastic and equal for all four.

Assuming that the engine has been stripped for decarbonizing the next step will be to remove the combined inlet and exhaust manifold together with the carburettor. For this, first release the air strangler wire from the carburettor by slackening its securing screw and disconnecting the throttle control by removing its retaining split pin. The unions of the petrol pipe from the pump to the carburettor must be detached at both ends, carefully

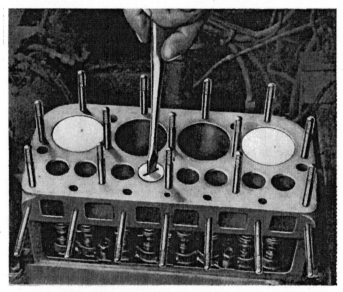

FIG. 50. GRINDING-IN THE VALVES

retaining their fibre washers and the gauze filter at the carburettor end.

Then disconnect the exhaust pipe from the manifold by undoing the four brass nuts. These nuts may present a little difficulty owing to the heat from the exhaust having distorted them to a slight extent.

The carburettor need not be separated from the manifold. The manifold and carburettor can be detached in one piece by undoing the seven brass securing nuts with their washers and drawing the manifold off the studs. There are two washers to take care of, the manifold joint washer and the exhaust pipe flange washer. These should both be examined and replaced if damaged or showing black areas where exhaust leaks have occurred.

The valve cover must next be removed by undoing its two

screws with large knurled heads. With the cover away, the valve springs, valve stems and tappets are visible. Using the thin tappet spanners out of the tool kit, slacken the locknuts of all the tappets and screw down the tappet heads to provide plenty of clearance for the subsequent operations. By using the valve spring compressor (Fig. 52) provided in the tool kit, taking one valve at a time, compress the coils of each spring and remove the split cotters and their cups. With all the cotters removed, take out all the eight valves, being careful to note their order. If it is desired to examine the valve springs they can be removed by partly compressing each with the compressor, and pulling them out slightly from the bottom to clear their respective tappets.

Examine all the valves in their order, and if none are too badly pitted they can be ground-in. If, however, pitting is pronounced the best plan is to have them refaced by a competent mechanic before grinding them in. Grinding-in involves rotating the valve head on its seating with a grinding compound in between.

Before commencing, carefully clean the valves of carbon and dip the stems in petrol and push them up and down in the guides to remove any gummy deposit.

If the valves are in a reasonable condition a fine grinding compound can be used. Otherwise use a coarse grade first and follow with the fine grade afterwards.

Smear the valve seating with a little compound and lower the valve.

Then rotate the valve backwards and forwards, using an even pressure on a screwdriver in the slotted head.

Make sure, when dealing with each valve, that the cams are well away from each tappet so that the valves can seat fully.

At intervals the valve receiving attention should be lifted off its seat (for this purpose a light spring placed under the valve head is of advantage) and replaced in a different position to evenly distribute the cutting compound and ensure a satisfactory seating for the complete circumference of the valve. Examine the valves as the work proceeds until a smooth dull ring is formed round the valve seat corresponding in width to the seat cut in the monobloc.

To test if the seat is true, clean all the compound from both valve and monobloc and replace. Then rotate the valve in this dry state as if continuing the grinding-in process. The correctly ground-in valve will then reveal a bright ring concentric with the smooth matt band first observed. If this ring is unbroken, the valve will be gas-tight on assembly. Proceed with grinding-in all the valves in this manner, taking each one in its proper order and grinding it in on its correct seat.

The exhaust valves will be found to take the longest time when grinding-in as they are manufactured from a steel having a tougher specification than that of the inlets. So see that they don't get mixed up.

Having correctly ground-in all the eight valves remove all traces of the grinding-in compound from them and from their seats on the monobloc. Make sure also that no compound has penetrated into the interior of the valve guides by repeating the

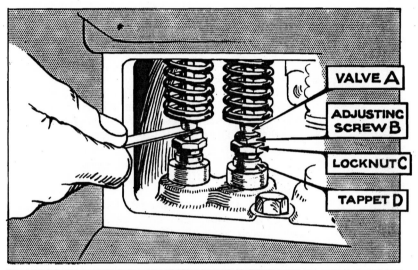

FIG. 51. TESTING TAPPET CLEARANCES

cleaning process of dipping the valve stems in petrol and passing them up and down the bores of the guides.

With everything perfectly clean, smear the valve stems with a little graphite grease for lubrication purposes and refit them to the monobloc, assembling the spring cup and split cotter with the aid of the valve spring compressor. The procedure is, of course, the reverse of that for dismantling. The split cotters may prove a little awkward to refit, but they will slip in place with a little patience and steady fingers. The next step is to adjust the tappets. Start from Number 1 valve and turning the engine with the starting handle watch it rise and fall. Then give the handle another quarter turn to ensure that the cam is well away from the base of the tappet. The first valve is then properly seated and the tappet head can be screwed up to the base of the valve stem; the necessary working clearance between them can be set with the gauge supplied in the tool kit.

The clearance provided by the use of the gauge is about

·004 in., and, having adjusted the tappet head to the gauge, lock it with the locknut provided, using the two thin tappet spanners.

After locking up this adjustment test the gap once more with the gauge (Fig. 51) to make sure that it has not been altered in the process. If it has shifted unlock the bottom nut, reset, and tighten the locknut again. On the Sports cars the tappet clearances are inlets, ·004 in. to ·006 in.; exhausts, ·006 in. to ·008 in.

FIG. 52. THE VALVE SPRING COMPRESSING TOOL IN ACTION

This procedure applies to all the eight valves from 1 to 8, ensuring in every case that the cam is well away from the base of the tappet of the valve concerned.

The most important work now completed, there only remains the refitting of the remaining dismantled parts. To accomplish this, simply reverse the order in which they were dismantled, taking particular care of the joint washers at the exhaust pipe flange, the manifold joint and the valve cover. The valve cover has a washer and must be fitted the right way up; it has breathing holes in its upper surface.

If the grinding-in process has been particularly well done the compression, when tested on the starting handle, will be up to standard. More often, however, it is not owing to the disturbance of the component parts of the engine.

If, however, the handle is tried again after the first short run, the true compression will be felt. After the first few miles have been run, remove the valve cover once more and check over the tappet clearances with the gauge. This is advised as the valves will have bedded down slightly in their seats.

Removing the Cylinders. If it is necessary to lift the cylinder block to gain access to the pistons, piston rings, and connecting rods, or for fitting a new tappet, tappet guide, or a valve guide, etc., the three nuts on the distributor side of the cylinder are easily removed, as are also the three barrel nuts on the valve side. They can be removed without difficulty when the valve cover has been taken off. For access to the nut at the front of the cylinder block the dynamo and casing with the fan bracket and fan must be lifted clear. First pull the ignition leads and the lead from the coil from their sockets in the distributor cover. Disconnect the dynamo, and remove the fan belt. The casing is secured by three setscrews and a nut. With the casing removed the front cylinder block nut is accessible. For access to the rear cylinder nut remove the inspection cover of the clutch pit from

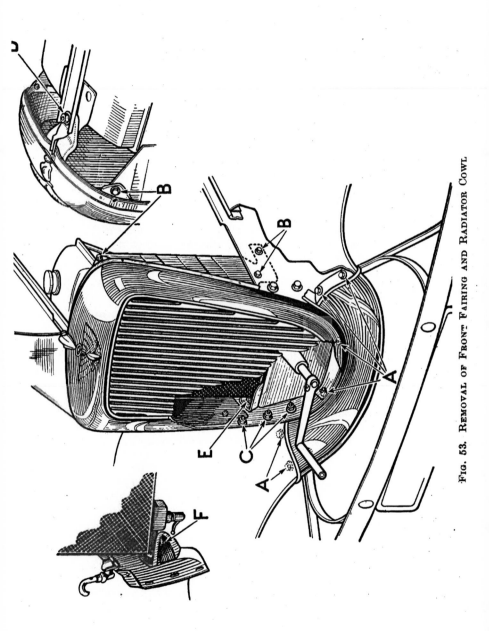

FIG. 53. REMOVAL OF FRONT FAIRING AND RADIATOR COWL

the toe-plate. Then remove the flywheel pit cover, which is secured by two setscrews to the flywheel housing. Remove the lower hose connection, and the cylinder block can be lifted. When refitting the cylinder block it is an advantage to use sleeves on the pistons to compress the rings. These piston ring sleeves are among the extra tools obtainable from the Service Department of the Austin Motor Co., Ltd. It will be necessary to re-time the ignition after re-assembling. (See page 115.)

Removal of Front Fairing and Radiator. To dismount the curved front fairing and/or the radiator, first remove the front bumper brackets and release the starting handle by undoing its securing bolt, then undo the six bolts (A, Fig. 53), all of which are accessible from beneath, and remove the fairing.

The two side plates can now be removed by undoing the three bolts B from each. The two at the bottom are passed through the flitch plates. Three bolts C secure either side of the cowl; remove these, and after lifting off the bonnet (see page 68) detach the bonnet support stay from its bracket by releasing bolt D, and free the cowl.

Now undo the two bolts E, one from either side of the radiator block and remove the front tray.

There now remain the two nuts F, one each side, holding the radiator block in its mountings. Remove these, having first taken out the split pins, and then slide down the spring and washer from each bolt. Take care of the felt mounting pads and replace them as before when re-assembling. Release both inlet and outlet hose connections and lift out the block. Re-assembling is a reversal of these instructions.

Clutch Relining. It was necessary, when relining the clutch of the preceding type of Austin Seven, completely to remove the engine and gearbox in one unit, afterwards detaching the gearbox from the dismantled unit.

The gearbox and flywheel of the latest type Austin Seven, however, can readily be withdrawn from inside the car, thereby effecting a considerable saving in time. To do this, push both front seats back as far as they will go and take out both the seat cushions; also remove the front rubber floor coverings. Then remove the nuts and bolts at A (Fig. 55), and the two setscrews at B, with their lock-washers, that together secure the gearbox draught and fume excluder, and the toe-plate above it, to the metal floor of the front compartment.

Then, working from underneath the car, fully slacken off the hand-brake lever adjustment and disconnect the speedometer coupling from the gearbox. Returning to the interior of the car, release the metal gearbox shield from the rubber seal round the base of the gear-lever. Then remove the shield by pulling it up

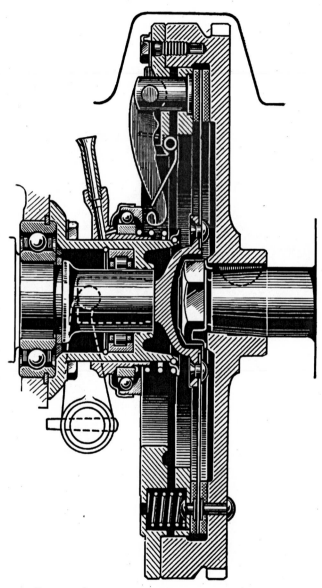

FIG. 54. SECTION OF THE AUSTIN SEVEN CLUTCH

and off the gear and hand-brake levers after pulling the latter right back. The rubber seal can be left on the base of the gear lever.

Leaving the interior, lift the offside of the bonnet and slacken the nuts and bolts securing the brake- and clutch-pedal stalks in the split ends of the levers. Returning to the front compartment, withdraw the pedal stalks through the toe-plate, being careful to

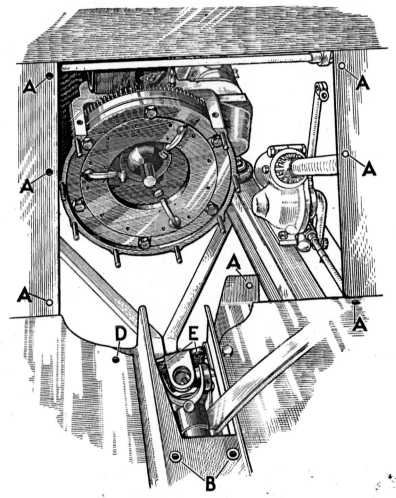

FIG. 55. THE GEARBOX OF THE 1936 AUSTIN SEVEN
CAN BE REMOVED FROM INSIDE THE CAR FOR
RELINING THE CLUTCH

retain the rubber and metal pedal washers on the engine side of the toe-plate. The toe-plate will then be free and can be removed.

Unlike the offside transmission tunnel body-bracket (which is riveted) the body-bracket on the nearside is bolted to the frame to allow it to be easily removed, which should be done next by undoing the three securing bolts to the frame, and a further bolt passing through the floor and a packing washer (see Fig. 56). The fibre packing piece shown in the illustration must be carefully retained and replaced when refitting this body bracket.

Bend back the lock-washer tangs of the four nuts and bolts at E (Fig. 55), securing the front propeller shaft joint to the third-motion shaft flange, unscrew the nuts, remove the four bolts, draw the joint back on its splines and allow the propeller shaft to rest on the hand-brake cross-shaft.

Next, remove the eight nuts and washers from the studs securing the gearbox to the flywheel housing, and the two set-screws retaining the metal flywheel pit cover.

It will then be possible to draw the gearbox off the studs and the splined clutch plate centre and lift it out of the car from the near side. The flywheel cover is then fully disclosed. It is secured by six setscrews and lock-washers. The flywheel cover should not be removed before first placing a special declutching lever retaining ring over the three toggle levers. This is to prevent the little mouse-trap springs fitted to the levers from being strained by the clutch springs as the flywheel cover securing setscrews are undone. To release the flywheel cover first knock back the lock-washer tangs with a blunt chisel and unscrew the six set-screws. With the retaining ring in position on the levers the cover and clutch pressure plate will come away from the flywheel and enable the clutch plate also to be removed. The next step is to remove the flywheel, the lining of which will have to be stripped off and a new one fitted. The flywheel is held on its keyed taper by a nut and lock-washer. Bend back the lock-washer tangs and unscrew the flywheel nut. To stop the flywheel from rotating while doing this place a bolt in one of the holes provided in the periphery of the flywheel. A flywheel extractor can be obtained together with the toggle lever retaining ring, from the Austin Motor Company. The extractor must be screwed into the two tapped holes in the flywheel which can then be pulled off.

The flywheel cover and the clutch pressure plate can now be separated; first removing the toggle lever springs. To do this, place the assembly in a vice and compress the cover and the pressure plate close to one of the three declutching lever pins. Do this very carefully, especially when refitting the springs after relining, because if the declutching lever pin is tight in its socket in the flywheel cover, the extra pressure necessary to compress the parts will very probably cause the base of the pin to crack the lining. The section of the clutch (Fig. 54) will show what is meant. The caution is unnecessary if the clutch lining is to be renewed, but if the clutch has been dismantled for some other reason, such as sticking declutching lever pins, the owner will not

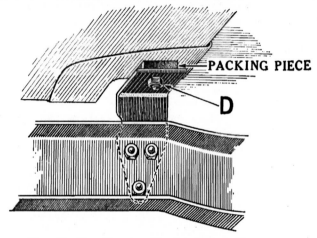

FIG. 56. THE PACKING PIECE MUST BE REPLACED
WHEN REFITTING BOLT *D*

be pleased if he finds that he has cracked a good lining by using too much pressure.

With the assembly compressed at the declutching lever pin it will be found that the lever spring can be removed. Be very careful not to strain these "mouse-trap" springs when dismantling or reassembling. It is a good plan to obtain one or two spare springs beforehand in case of accident. Remove the two remaining springs in turn, compressing the assembly together in the vice close to each declutching lever pin.

When all three springs have been removed, the retaining ring, which was placed on the levers before the flywheel cover was removed from the flywheel, can be removed and put aside.

Place the assembly on the bench with the clutch pressure plate down and the flywheel cover can then be separated from the pressure plate by threading the declutching levers through the holes in the cover. Carefully retain the twelve clutch springs that are now revealed; a good plan is to string them up and hang them on a nail in the garage until the relining has been completed.

While the clutch is dismantled make quite sure that the

declutching lever withdrawal pins are not sticking in their sockets in the flywheel cover. If necessary take each pin in turn and polish it with a slip of emery cloth; the same can be done to their respective sockets.

The old linings on the pressure plate and inside the flywheel can easily be stripped off and the new ones riveted on in their place. The shaped and drilled linings and the aluminium rivets can be bought ready to fit on. The lining on the flywheel is held by twelve rivets, and it should be ensured that the heads of the rivets are well below the surface of the linings. It will be noted that the lining on the pressure plate holds the declutching lever withdrawal pins in place so see that the pins are in position before riveting up the new lining. Twelve rivets likewise secure the pressure plate lining, and similarly it should be ensured that the rivet heads are not left proud of the surface of the lining.

Place the pressure plate on the bench, lining downwards, and reassemble the flywheel cover with the twelve clutch springs between them.

Then press the flywheel cover down, compressing the twelve springs, and fit the declutching lever retaining ring previously described. Next, refit the three toggle lever springs. Grip the flywheel cover and the pressure plate in the vice close to a withdrawal pin and tighten up. The declutching lever spring can then be manipulated into position. These springs are sometimes awkward to remove and to refit, and a pair of round-nosed pliers may be used with advantage. Refit all three springs in this way, being careful not to crack the new lining.

The relined flywheel can be refitted on its keyed taper on the end of the crankshaft, the lock-washer and nut replaced, the flywheel prevented from turning by the bolt in its periphery, and the flywheel nut tightened up hard. Turn up the tangs of lock-washer and be careful to remove the loose bolt from the flywheel edge afterwards.

Then replace the clutch plate; it will rest against the lining, and offer up the assembled flywheel cover after giving the levers and withdrawal pins a drop of oil. Fit, and partly screw up, each of the six setscrews through the cover into the flywheel, not forgetting their lock-washers, and remove the retaining ring from the levers.

The next part of the procedure is important. The splined clutch plate centre must be accurately centred before attempting to replace the gearbox. A special centring plate, as shown in Fig. 57, can be obtained for this purpose from the Austin Motor Company.

The two outer holes in the plate fit over two opposite studs on the flywheel housing. The clutch plate centre is then located in the middle hole in the plate, while the six flywheel cover set-screws are finally tightened home. The clutch plate centre has one spline missing for location purposes. Refitting the gearbox is rendered easier if this gap in the splines is on top centre.

With the clutch centre perfectly central and the six flywheel cover setscrews fully secured, the centring plate can be removed and the lock-washer tangs turned up. Now turn to the gearbox

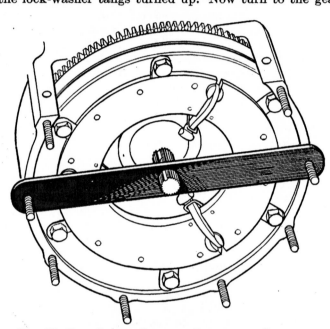

FIG. 57. THIS CLUTCH CENTRING BAR CAN BE OBTAINED FROM THE AUSTIN MOTOR CO. LTD.

and put the gear lever into top gear and rotate the first motion shaft flange until the splined part corresponding to the missing spline on the clutch plate centre is also on top centre. Then care-fully mark the rear of the gearbox and the third motion shaft flange, and also loosen the bolt securing the clutch pedal lever to the spindle. It is necessary to have the clutch pedal lever loose in this manner to prevent it fouling the steering box when manoeuvring the gearbox into position inside the car. The gear box is now ready to go inside the car and be offered up to the housing. This last stage takes a little wangling and patience.

First get the gearbox clutch-bearing housing over the clutch plate centre and the rear of the gearbox down well below the level of the transmission tunnel. Now draw back the gearbox and place the first motion shaft and the clutch plate centre in line. If you tire of holding the gearbox it can be rested on the chassis.

Assuming that the gearbox is level, turn the third motion shaft until the mark made on it corresponds with the mark made on the gearbox. If the gear lever is still in top this should bring the missing spline and its counterpart in line, so that with a little persuasion the gearbox will slide forward, the clutch plate centre will locate with the first motion shaft flange, and the holes in the gearbox flange will encircle the studs in the flywheel housing. Then fit and screw up the eight nuts and washers on the studs, and replace the flywheel pit cover (two setscrews). Refitting the other parts is simply a reversal of the dismantling process already described. When the reassembly is complete, adjust the clutch pedal to give about 1 in. free movement.

Brakes. A virtue of the Austin Seven that is not fully realized by owners until a considerable mileage has been covered, is the ease with which the efficiency of the braking system can be maintained. A very important point, this, as the braking system must always be as dependable as the car.

The hand lever and pedal of the new car will be found, like the clutch pedal, to have a certain amount of free movement. This ensures that the brake shoes are not rubbing against their drums when out of action. The gradual wear of the brake linings as the brakes are used will, of course, increase the amount of lost movement in the levers. The linings give lengthy service for a slight amount of wear, but that wear is magnified at the levers, by the ratio of the mechanical leverage of the system ; so that the unwanted lost movement at the pedal and hand-brake levers has to be taken up on occasion by the means of adjustment.

The 1937 series cars have brakes with steel shoes and Girling type adjusters. Each brake can be adjusted to a given clearance and it is unnecessary to jack up the car to do so. Screwing in the adjuster cone forces apart the shoes on to the interior surface of the drum ; when the resistance is felt, turn the adjuster back a quarter turn. This provides about 0·003 in. clearance between the shoes and the drum.

Adjustment of the superseded system can be readily effected by turning, in a clockwise direction looking from the rear, the winged nut shown in Fig. 45. This nut is reached by raising a disc in the floor in front of the driver's seat. Pull on the hand-brake—this enables the wing nut to be turned easily.

The best procedure is to turn the nut by a small amount, say half a turn, and then try the feel of the brake pedal, making any further adjustment to suit.

A wing nut at the base of the hand lever on the hand-brake adjusting lever provides independent adjustment for this control.

To make the adjustment and take up the slack between the hand lever and the brake gear, turn the wing nut clockwise until approximately an inch of free movement is felt at the top of the hand lever or about one notch on the ratchet (see Fig. 25).

It may happen after considerable service that one set of brake shoe linings will wear down more rapidly than its fellows, or the rear brakes may come on before the front. In either case it will be necessary to equalize or compensate the system.

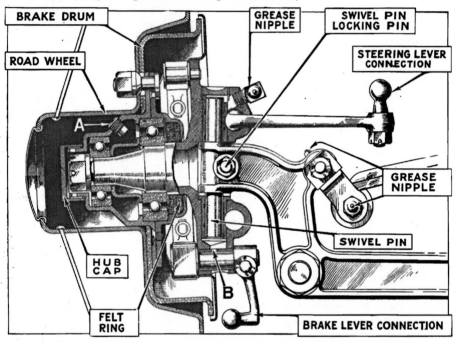

FIG. 58. THE FRONT BRAKE DRUM AND HUB IN SECTION Pre-1937
B shows how the brake cam spindle is lubricated from the swivel pin greaser

The cable actuating the front brakes automatically compensates them. To test the brakes jack the car up off all four wheels, depress the foot pedal so that the brakes are on, but not hard on, by using a piece of wood of suitable length between the brake pedal and the base of the driver's seat. Then grasp each road wheel and endeavour to rotate them in turn.

The set of brake shoes that have worn more than the others will be readily detected by the amount of resistance met when attempting to turn the corresponding wheel or wheels.

If the rear brake shoes are erring they can be equalized by the individual adjustment provided on each cable.

A screwed end, attached to the cable, screws into the front fork end at the compensating tube lever. If the fork end is removed from the lever by detaching the pin that holds it, the fork can be screwed either on or off the screwed cable end to effect the adjustment. The cable must not be twisted while this is being done, and always adjust the hand-brake after dealing with the pedal adjusting nut.

When all the wheels offer an equal resistance to turning the brakes are compensated and will come on together when the car is braked on the road.

By making these adjustments from time to time as occasioned

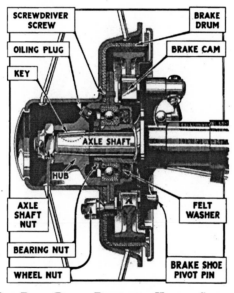

FIG. 59. THE REAR BRAKE DRUM AND HUB IN SECTION Pre-1937

by the wear taken from the brake linings, the system can be maintained as an efficient and dependable part of the car.

The time will come, however, on the earlier Sevens when the linings will wear down to render inadequate the range of adjustment described. The brake linings will then need to be renewed.

To do this first jack up all four wheels and let the hand-brake right off. Remove all four road wheels and then remove each brake drum by unscrewing the three screws securing each to their respective hubs.

Remove the front hub caps, screw on the extractor, and remove the plug *A* from the hub (Fig. 58), otherwise it will foul the outer bearing when the hub is being extracted. Draw off the outer portion of the hub. The axle nut and split pin will then be accessible for removal. Remove them and then replace the outer portion of the hub and pull it to its original position by the wheel nuts. Then draw off the hub complete with its bearing and packing with the extractor. The brake shoes are now clear for removal. On reassembling remember to fit a new split pin through the axle and nut.

For the rear wheel hubs (Fig. 59) remove the axle shaft nut, having first taken out the split pin, and extract the outer portion of the hub with the extractor. Next remove the bearing nut, having knocked back the tang of the washer locking it. Re-fit

FIG. 60. THE REAR HUB WITH BRAKE
DRUM REMOVED Pre-1937

the outer half as closely as possible, using the wheel nuts to draw the two halves together. Then use the hub extractor a second time, and so remove the hub together with bearing and packing between the hub and the felt housing faces. When re-fitting always use a new paper washer, as it is important to make a good joint on reassembling, to prevent the hub lubricant penetrating to the brake linings. The brake shoes can then be pulled off the cam and pivot pin, and the springs unhooked.

Each shoe can be dealt with in turn, first punching out the retaining rivets and discarding the old linings and then clamping the new shaped lining to the shoe while the rivet holes are drilled.

It is best to clamp the lining to the shoe by gripping both horizontally in a vice and drilling the linings one side at a time through the holes in the shoe. If one side is done at a time pegs can be used to secure the drilled lining to the corresponding side of the shoe so that the shoe and lining can be turned over and resecured in the vice ready for drilling the outer side without disturbing their relative positions.

When the rivet holes have been drilled in the linings they should be countersunk enough to allow the head of the rivet to be, when riveted, about $\frac{3}{32}$ in. below the surface of the brake lining. If this is not done properly, the rivets may work proud of the lining

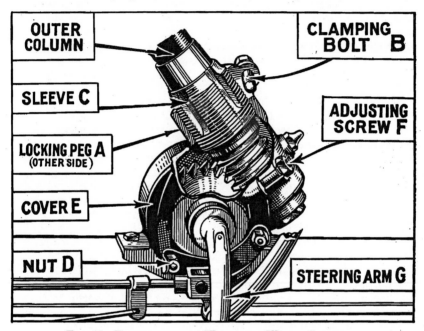

FIG. 61. DETAILS OF THE WORM AND WHEEL STEERING

or the lining may wear down to the rivets and cause bad braking and probable scoring of the brake drums.

After riveting the linings on to the shoes they should be bevelled along the edges with a coarse file and the ends backed off with the same tool to provide leading and trailing edges to ensure that the brakes do not "grab" when applied.

The amount of backing need not be much. The ends can be filed back, starting from the surface of the lining at the first rivet down to about half the thickness of the lining at the ends. Reassembly is a reversal of the process described above, all adjustment must, of course, be restored before the hubs and drums can be refitted. Don't forget to split-pin the castellated axle shaft nuts.

When the wheels have been refitted it will be necessary to compensate or equalize the sets of shoes again in the manner previously described.

After about a hundred miles have been done since the brakes were relined it is a good plan to jack up all the wheels again and equalize the front and rear brakes once more as they may have settled down a little unevenly.

Steering. The steering is affected considerably by the pressure of air in the tyres. The habit should be formed of periodically testing the tyre pressures with a gauge. The front and rear tyres should have about the same pressures to minimize wear.

For all models the correct tyre pressures are 22 lb. per sq. in. in front and rear and 26 lb. per sq. in. at the rear if the car is fully laden.

Steering wander on the Seven may be due to a slack front spring anchorage. The four "U" bolt nuts must be tight.

If slackness is present in the steering two adjustments are available: To take up the play in the column, loosen the nut which tightens the bracket supporting the steering outer column to the instrument board, unscrew the locking peg (A), Fig. 61, and the clamping bolt (B), and turn the sleeve (C) with the special spanner provided for the purpose, until the play has been removed. The steering will be stiff if the sleeve is screwed in too tight. Having adjusted the sleeve correctly, re-fit the locking peg so that it enters one of the slots of the sleeve, tighten up the clamping bolt, and the supporting bracket at the instrument board. Excessive play between the worm and worm wheel, due to wear, can be taken up by unlocking the locking plates and slackening the three nuts (D), holding the cover (E) to the worm casing. Then turn the adjusting screw (F) slightly to draw the cover in the direction of the worm. Carefully ensure that the worm wheel is not brought too tightly into mesh with the worm or it will make the steering stiff. Tighten up the three nuts (D) and lock them with the locking plates after effecting the adjustment.

THE FUEL SYSTEM

The Petrol Pump. The petrol pump which delivers the fuel in the correct quantity demanded by the carburettor, possesses an automatic mechanism which accurately governs the operation.

The revolving camshaft (G) with the eccentric (H) lifts the rocker arm (D), which is pivoted at (E) and which pulls the pull rod (F), together with the diaphragm (A) downward against pressure of the spring (C), so causing a vacuum to be created in the pump chamber (M).

Fuel from the tank at the rear of the car will enter at (J) into the sediment chamber (K) and pass through the filter gauze (L) and the suction valve (N) into the pump chamber (M). On the return stroke, spring pressure (C) pushes the diaphragm (A)

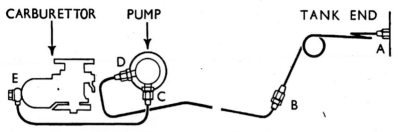

CARBURETTOR   PUMP   TANK END

E   A
                    D
                    C   B

Fig. 62. Diagram of the Fuel System

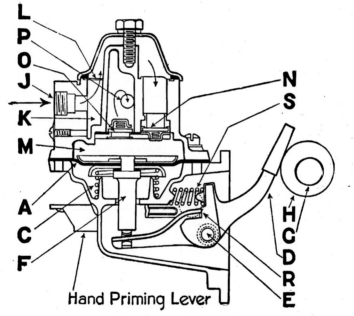

L
P
O
J
K
M
                                                               N
                                                               S

A   H
C   C
F   D
                                                               R
Hand Priming Lever   E

Fig. 63. The Petrol Pump in Section

upwards, forcing the fuel from the chamber (M) through the pressure valve (O) and the opening (P) into the carburettor.

When the carburettor bowl is filled the float in the float chamber shuts off the inlet needle valve, thus creating a back pressure in the pump chamber (M). This pressure will hold the diaphragm (A) downward against the spring pressure (C), and it will remain in this position until the carburettor requires further fuel. The float then descends and opens the needle valve. The rocker arm (D) is in two parts, the outer operating the inner by making contact at (R) and the movement of the eccentric (H) is absorbed by this "break" when fuel is not required.

The spring (S) is merely for the purpose of keeping the rocker arm (D) in constant contact with the eccentric (H) to eliminate noise.

No regular maintenance attentions are required by this pump. It is a self-contained unit that will, in all probability, function faultlessly for years without attention by the owner. It is designed to operate without adjustment of the moving parts and without lubrication. The latter is provided for by oily vapour from the crankcase which lubricates the linkage below the diaphragm.

If attention is likely to be demanded it will doubtless resolve into an occasional clean for the gauze filter under the cover in the head of the pump.

To do this remove the top cover by undoing its securing screw. The gauze lies immediately below and can be removed for cleaning by rinsing in petrol.

The main chamber of the pump is now exposed, and the opportunity should be taken to swill out any foreign matter that may be present, before refitting the gauze. Locate the holes for the centre screw and the pump inlet valve correctly when replacing the gauze and also see that the top cover makes a good fit on its cork washer to obviate the possibility of subsequent leakage.

Leakage of fuel from the pump can arise from other reasons than the one mentioned above. The inlet and the outlet pipe unions must be kept tight, and leakage from the diaphragm itself will arise if the five diaphragm screws round the pump casting flange are not screwed up tight.

The fuel pump is not necessarily always to blame if flooding occurs at the carburettor; more often than not this is due to grit preventing the float chamber needle from seating properly. (See page 94.) (This needle controls the output of the pump to the carburettor.) If, however, it is apparent that the pump is not providing an adequate supply of fuel to the carburettor, the cause of the trouble will probably lie in the pump valves. To inspect the valves, the best plan is to remove the petrol pump from the crankcase. To attempt to remove the valves without doing so is not easy and may result in damaging them.

The pump is easily removed, first disconnecting the inlet and outlet delivery pipe unions and then undoing the two nuts securing the pump to the crankcase.

The pump can now be taken to the garage bench and the inlet and outlet valves removed. These are just under the gauze ; they can both be easily removed. The valve springs and the valves may be emptied out into the palm of the hand, being careful not to mix them up; the outlet valve spring locates round the stem of the valve and round the short stem on the inside of the valve plug.

Examine the valves and their seatings and see that foreign matter is not preventing the valves from seating properly.

If either valves are damaged replace with new ones and clean

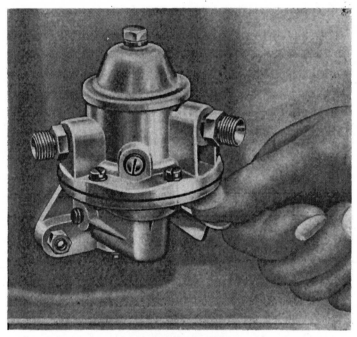

FIG. 64. THE HAND PRIMING LEVER OF THE LATEST TYPE PETROL PUMP

their seatings before refitting. When replacing the outlet valve plug ensure that its stem locates in the coils of the valve spring which has previously been replaced on top of the valve. The same applies to the inlet valve except that its spring is beneath the actual valve plate.

It is important that the fibre washers under the heads of both valve plugs are not omitted on reassembly and also ensure that both plugs are tight home. There is also a fibre washer under the head of the top cover screw.

The linkage operating the diaphragm will not require attention, and in nearly every case the only necessary attention to the pump will be a cursory examination of the gauze filter under the top cover.

The Carburettor. From the rear tank the petrol flows via the pump through the union (*A*), (Fig. 65), the filter and the needle seating into the float chamber. The petrol rises, and when reaching a certain predetermined height causes the float to push the needle on to its seating, thus regulating the petrol flow.

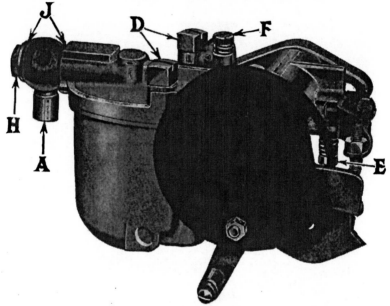

FIG. 65. THE ZENITH CARBURETTOR FITTED TO THE
AUSTIN SEVEN

The float chamber contains the main jet (1), (Fig. 66), compensating jet (2), compensating well (3), and slow running jet (4). The petrol then flows through the main and compensating jets and also rises in the compensating well.

From the jets the petrol flows along two separate channels into a common channel in the emulsion block (5), which is attached to the float chamber.

The petrol in the compensating well is in direct communication with the air and with the emulsion block. Consequently, all the petrol from the jets and compensating well is centred in one channel in the emulsion block. This channel leads to a nozzle (6), which projects directly into the choke tube.

Starting. To obtain an easy start from cold the control on the dash operating the air strangler should be fully extended and the engine should be cranked over a few times by pulling out the self-starter control knob.

Then release the knob to the first notch, which partially opens

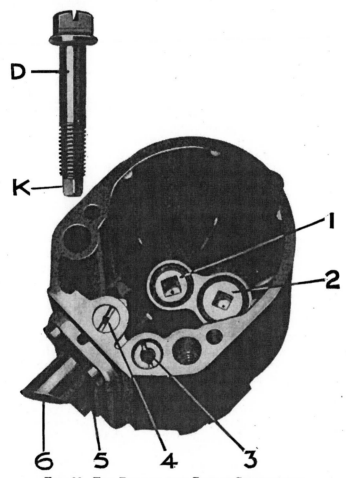

FIG. 66. THE BASE OF THE ZENITH CARBURETTOR

D = Holding down screw	*K* = Squared end to form jet key
1 = Main jet	4 = Slow-running jet
2 = Compensating jet	5 = Emulsion block
3 = Compensating well	6 = Nozzle

the air strangler, and opens the throttle a little. If the engine is then switched on it should start readily and continue to run.

It is quite in order to run for a short while with the knob in the first notch, thus temporarily enriching the mixture and assisting the get away from cold. Then, as the engine warms up, release to the second notch, until, in a few minutes, the engine has reached a reasonable temperature, when the knob can be pushed right in.

Difficulty can be caused by the strangler flap not closing properly, and the control wires should be examined, and if necessary, altered, to permit the flap closing fully. A choked slow-running jet will also cause difficulty, and this part should be taken out of the carburettor, and carefully cleaned.

Trouble can also be caused if the throttle is not opening sufficiently when the strangler knob on the dash is in the first notch, and in this case turning the screw (E) a little to the right will have the effect of opening the throttle a little wider.

If the mixture for slow running is weak, this can also cause difficulty in starting up, and in this case turn the regulating screw (F) in a clockwise direction, which will enrich the mixture for starting and slow running, but do not overdo this, as if the mixture is too rich, the engine will hunt and tend to choke when running slowly with the engine warm.

Adjustments. The carburettor is delivered with the setting that has been found by extensive experimental work to be most suitable. Consequently, very little adjustment to the carburettor is needed. Indeed, the user will find that a greater service will be obtained from the carburettor if the various screws, etc., are only moved when absolutely necessary.

On those occasions, however, when an adjustment is advisable (after a new car has been "run-in" an adjustment of the slow running is sometimes necessary, or when the carburettor requires cleaning), the following procedure should be observed.

There are two adjustments for the slow running which may need attention. One is the throttle stop screw, which, unless too stiff, can be turned with the fingers. This screw determines how far the throttle can be closed. By turning it in a clockwise direction it increases the minimum degree of opening, turned anti-clockwise a slower tick-over is obtained. The other slow-running adjustment at F regulates the strength of the slow-running mixture by varying the suction. Turned anti-clockwise the strength of the mixture is weakened, turned clockwise it is strengthened.

Both these adjustments should be effected when the engine is warm after a run. The combined adjustments should give a good pick-up without a falter when the throttle is snapped open and a steady even tick-over when the throttle is released. If the engine refuses to tick-over for any length of time, or it stalls on deceleration it is a sure sign that the slow-running mixture is weak. To remedy this the mixture should be enriched by turning the regulating screw (F) in a clockwise direction.

If, however, the engine hunts when idling, the mixture is too

rich and requires weakening by turning the air regulating screw
(*F*) anti-clockwise.

Poor Acceleration. In the winter time this can be very often due
to the engine not getting sufficiently hot.

If, in spite of the engine being thoroughly hot, the acceleration
is bad, then see to the following points.

Slow-running Adjustment is Too Weak. Try the screw (*F*)
in a richer position. *The compensating jet "2" is too small*—Try
one size larger.

Lack of Power and Speed. If this is due to the carburettor it
is probably owing to the main jet being partially choked or a
little too small, and a size larger should be tried. Care should be
taken to make sure the lack of speed is not due to the ignition
being retarded or to an insufficient supply of petrol, from the tank,
faulty ignition, or too poor compression due to leaking valves or
wrong tappet adjustment.

Make sure also, that the strangler valve opens fully, as if this
sticks in a partially closed position it will restrict the speed of the
car and increase petrol consumption.

Dismantling the Carburettor. The bowl of the carburettor
can be removed by taking out the holding-down screws (*D*).
The hand should be placed underneath the bowl during this
operation, for when the screws are removed the bowl will drop
into the hand, and any petrol that is contained in the bowl can
then be emptied back into the tank. On turning the bowl
upside down the float will slide out and reveal the main and compensating jets at the bottom of the bowl. (See Fig. 66.)

The Jets. The jets should be removed occasionally and be
thoroughly cleaned. The holding-down screws (*D*) are shaped
at the end to fit into the jets. When the bottom end is placed
into the jets a spanner applied to the head of the screw will loosen
the jets for removal.

When cleaning the jets it is not advisable to pass any wire
through them that is liable to damage them. The most satisfactory and effective method is to blow through the jets and wash
them in petrol. This will remove any obstruction and leave the
jets undamaged.

The sizes of all jets in Zenith carburettors run in numbers—the
larger the number the larger is the jet.

The Filter. The petrol is filtered on entering the carburettor,
and the filter should be cleaned from time to time. To remove
the filter unscrew the petrol connection *H* and pull the filter
out of its chamber. The filter gauze can then be thoroughly
cleaned with petrol.

When reassembling the filter, care must be taken to see that
the washers (*J*) are correctly replaced.

Alteration of the Standard Adjustment. The complete standard setting for this carburettor is shown below—

Choke tube	.	.	.	17
Main jet	.	.	.	57
Compensating jet	.	.	.	50
Slow running jet	.	.	.	60
Capacity tube	.	.	.	2
Progression jet	.	.	.	100

When you have any trouble with your engine do not assume

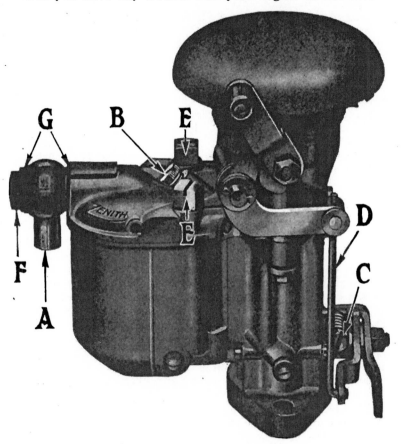

FIG. 67. THE ZENITH CARBURETTOR FITTED TO SPORTS CARS IS OF THE DOWN-DRAUGHT TYPE

that it is always due to the carburettor. Check the carburettor first of all for cleanliness and make sure that the setting is in accordance with the standard mentioned.

If these are found correct then do not be tempted to alter the carburettor until you have gone over all other likely parts of the engine, such as the sparking plugs, ignition timing, the valves may be sticking, and things of that kind, because there are no moving parts in connection with the adjustment of the Zenith carburettor, and consequently the adjustment cannot alter of its own accord.

If the engine suddenly starts to run badly, this cannot be caused by faulty carburation, providing all the passages and jets are clear and there is a good supply of petrol from the tank.

The carburettor fitted to the Sports Models is of the down-draught type (Fig. 67). It embodies the well-known Zenith principles of main and compensating jets. The carburettor is mounted on top of the inlet pipe, because the fundamental advantage of down-draught carburation lies in the fact that fuel is assisted by gravity into the cylinders, instead of having to be lifted against it as is the case of a normal vertical instrument.

One of the holding-down screws is squared at the end and can be used to remove the jets.

A small screwdriver will remove the slow-running jet. When cleaning the jets, do not pass anything through them that is likely to damage the carefully calibrated orifices. The most satisfactory and efficient method is to blow through them and wash them in petrol. Swill out with a little petrol any sediment which may have collected in the bottom of the float chamber. It is not necessary to remove the emulsion block from the float chamber. Unscrew the petrol pipe connection F, and withdraw the filter gauze. Thoroughly clean this part by washing in petrol. When reassembling the filter care must be taken to see that the washers G are correctly replaced.

Adjustments. The carburettor is delivered with the setting that has been found by extensive experimental work to be most suitable for all-round conditions. The complete standard setting is as follows—

	Nippy	Speedy
Choke tube	21	25
Main jet	85	120
Compensating jet . . .	55	40
Slow-running jet . . .	60	60
Capacity tube . . .	2	2
Progression jet . . .	90	90

The main jet has the greatest influence at high engine speeds, therefore alteration of this jet would affect maximum power and road speed.

Compensating Jet. This jet has a controlling effect upon acceleration from low speeds, low speed pulling on hills, and quick "get-away" from cold.

The Slow-running Jet. This jet measures the petrol supplied when the engine is idling. Petrol is drawn through this jet into a channel which has its outlet at the throttle edge. The petrol is atomized immediately on leaving the jet by air entering the carburettor at the base of the slow-running adjusting screw. The size of slow-running jet should be such that smooth regular idling is provided with the slow-running screw *B* set approxi-

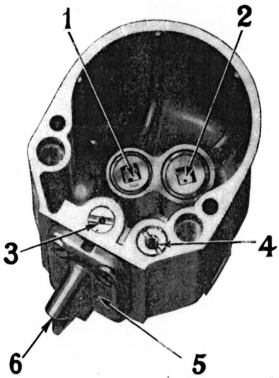

Fig. 68. The Base of the Zenith Down-draught
Type Carburettor

1 = Main jet	4 = Compensating well
2 = Compensating jet	5 = Emulsion block
3 = Slow-running jet	6 = Nozzle

mately one complete turn open. This adjustment should always be made with the engine quite hot. The speed at which the engine idles can be regulated by means of the throttle arm stop-screw *C*. Turning this part in a clockwise direction increases the engine speed and *vice versa*. In all cases of difficulty with slow running, inspect the slow-running jet for obstruction, and check the position of the screws *B* and *C*. Continued difficulty may be traced to air leaks at inlet pipe joints, etc., to the valves, or to the ignition system.

Starting from Cold. Easy starting with the VE1 carburettor is assured by an automatic air strangler interconnected with the throttle lever. The strangler is situated in the air intake of the carburettor, and is closed by fully extending the dashboard control. By means of the interconnection mechanism, this operation sets the throttle open just the right amount to ensure an easy start.

To avoid the possibility of the strangler permitting excessively rich mixture passing into the cylinders, a diaphragm has been embodied in the strangler flap, which will open and permit extra air to enter immediately the engine fires. The quick opening and closing of this diaphragm when the engine is running will cause a buzzing noise, and this serves to remind the driver that the strangler is still in operation and should be released. A half-way position is provided on the dashboard control, and it is advisable to run the engine for a few minutes during cold weather with the strangler in this position, before attempting to drive the car away.

Failure to Start Readily. The carburettor having been cleaned and the ignition system, valves, etc., checked over, the following points should be examined.

Make sure the air strangler flap closes completely when the dashboard control is operated and ascertain that petrol is being supplied to the float chamber by the fuel pump.

After lengthy service it may become necessary to readjust the interconnection between strangler and throttle; shortening the connecting link D will increase the opening of the throttle.

When cars are used in very hot climates or at high altitudes, a slightly weaker setting than normal is usually required.

CHAPTER VII

Ignition. The coil ignition system is provided with an automatic advance mechanism, which relieves the driver of the necessity of constant adjustment of a hand ignition control. Its advantages are particularly evident when accelerating, and during hill climbing, pre-ignition, knocking, or "pinking" being very much reduced.

The device is housed in the distributor body, and it consists of a centrifugally-operated mechanism by means of which the ignition is advanced in proportion to the engine speed.

Very little attention is needed to keep the ignition equipment in first rate condition if the following instructions on lubrication, cleaning, and adjustment are carried out.

The Distributor. The distributor cover can be removed on springing aside its two securing clips. The electrodes B and H, Fig. 69, and the inside of the cover are then accessible for cleaning with a dry duster. See that the carbon brush A is clean and moves freely in its holder. The contact breaker points can be similarly cleaned if required. Normally the gap between the contacts will not require adjustment until a considerable mileage has been covered, unless the points have burned. For this adjustment, first turn the engine by the starting handle until the points are seen to be fully open. Then, using the ignition screwdriver, slacken the two screws D in the contact plate, and move the plate until the gap is set to the thickness of the gauge. After making the adjustment care must be taken to tighten the locking screws.

The Coil. The coil needs no attention apart from keeping the terminals tight and the top clean.

Ignition Switch and Warning Lamp. The key by means of which the ignition is switched on should be withdrawn when the engine is not running; this will ensure that the battery does not discharge by the current continuing to flow through the coil windings.

The warning lamp on the instrument panel will light when the ignition is switched on and the engine is not running. Should the bulb of the warning lamp fail, this will not affect the ignition, but it should be replaced as soon as possible. It can be removed from its socket when the small cover plate holding the red glass is unsrewed. The replacement bulb should be a 2·5 volt, ·2 amp. screw cap type (No. 252 M.E.S.) as originally fitted.

Lubrication. The distributor spindle bearing is lubricated by means of an oiler which needs a few drops of oil every 1,000 miles. Every 3,000 miles, give the cam the slightest smear of vaseline and place a single drop of oil on the pivot *J* on which the contact breaker works. Withdraw the rotating arm *G* from the top of the spindle by lifting it off, and add a few drops of thin oil to the top of the spindle. Do not remove the screw exposed to view,

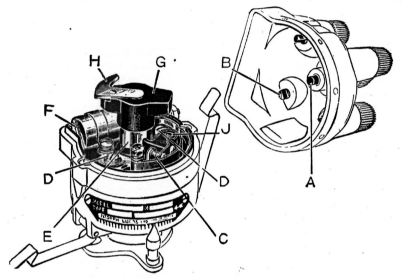

FIG. 69. PART SECTIONAL VIEW OF THE DISTRIBUTOR

as there is a clearance between the screw and the inner face of the spindle through which the oil passes to lubricate the automatic timing control. Take care to refit the arm correctly and to push it on to the shaft as far as possible.

High-tension Leads. When the high-tension cables show signs of perishing or cracking, they should be replaced. Use only 7 mm. rubber-covered ignition cable for all high-tension leads.

To make a connection to the distributor or coil terminals, thread the knurled insulating nut over the lead, bare the end of the cable for about ¼ in., thread the wire through the brass washer provided, and bend the strands back. When the moulded nut is screwed home, the cable will be securely clamped, and the nut will support the cable, and prevent vibration and fracture.

Ignition Faults. When the engine will not fire, or fires erratically, the trouble may arise from the carburettor, or petrol supply, and not the ignition. A partially choked jet, an incorrect petrol level, or air leaks into the induction system may be the cause. Equally, sooted plugs can be suspected, when dismantling and cleaning them will remedy the trouble. If the battery is run down or its terminals have worked loose, quite obviously there will be no spark, and the same can be expected if the distributor electrodes and contact breaker have been neglected and are dirty.

The coil can be tested by removing the cable from the centre socket on the distributor cover, and holding the end of this cable about ¼ in. from some metal part of the car, while the ignition switch is on and the engine is turned. A strong and regular spark will result if the coil is in order. Clean the top of the coil, and ensure that its terminals are tight before making this test.

To test for short circuits in the low-tension wiring (the cables from the switchboard to coil, coil to distributor, and distributor to chassis, which would equally cause irregular running), have the engine turned over by hand while the ignition is switched on, and watch the ammeter reading. It should rise and fall as the contact breaker points close and open. This test will also indicate if the contact breaker is functioning correctly. If the contacts remain open, there will be no discharge, if partially closed the reading will fluctuate.

If the high-tension cables from the distributor to the plugs are not securely attached to the distributor, misfiring may occur. Or, if the rubber insulation shows signs of perishing, there may be leakage of current giving rise to the same symptoms. Renewing the cables is then the remedy.

Sparking Plugs. The modern sparking plug is a dependable item of the ignition system. Many owners will be surprised to know that for every mile traversed by their car, each plug functions at least 1,500 times.

The plugs will benefit by an occasional inspection and clean. They should receive this attention every time the engine is decarbonized, at least. They are easily dismantled by gripping the small gland-nut hexagon in the vice and unscrewing the body of the plug from the insulated centre by using a box spanner on the larger hexagon. This must be done carefully to avoid damaging the mica insulation.

A petrol rag will remove any gummy deposit from the lower insulation and the lower interior of the earthing shell. All traces of carbon must also be removed from the plug points and the interior of the plug body. The parts may then be washed in petrol and carefully reassembled, care being taken to replace the internal copper joint-washer under the plug centre before fully tightening the gland nut. Then set the plug points to the thick blade of the gauge supplied with the tool-kit, or if the gauge is not available, set the points to ·020 in. When refitting the cleaned plugs in the engine see that the copper-asbestos washers are in

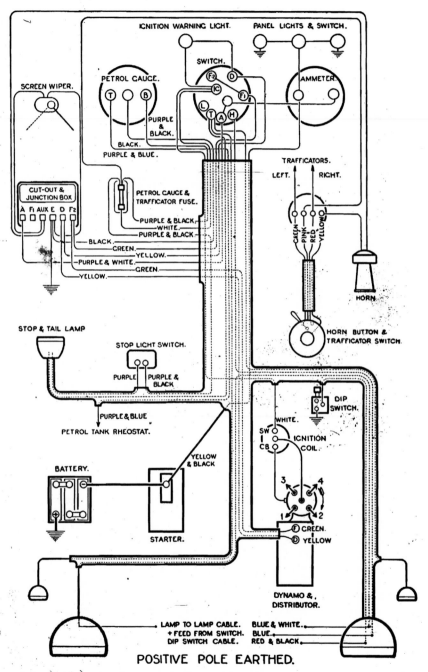

FIG. 70. AUSTIN SEVEN WIRING DIAGRAM

place. If these washers have been pressed flat it will be as well to replace them with new ones and so obviate the possibility of gas leaks round the plugs.

THE LAMPS

Headlamps. The headlamps of the Austin Seven are provided with an electrically-operated anti-dazzle device for operation by a foot switch. When the switch is operated by the driver's left foot, the near-side headlamp beam is dipped and turned to the near-side of the road, while at the same time, the off-side headlamp is switched off, thus causing no discomfort to approaching traffic.

The dipping of the headlamp beam is effected by a movement of the lamp reflector. This is made in two parts; the centre portion is pivoted in a fixed rim which is in turn secured to the body. Movement of the reflector is controlled by means of a solenoid and plunger which, when the current is switched on, tilts the reflector to give the dipped beam.

Removing the Lamp Front and Reflector. To remove the lamp front, slacken the fixing screw at the bottom of the lamp and swing it aside from the slot. The front can then be withdrawn. When replacing, press the front on to the lamp body, locating the top of the rim first. Finally, swing the screw into the slot and tighten it to lock the front into position.

To remove the near-side reflector, withdraw the fixing screw at the back of the lamp. The reflector can then be withdrawn by dislocating the tongues of the two fixing brackets riveted to the reflector rim from the slots in the lamp body. The offside reflector can be removed together with the front.

Focusing and Alining. To obtain the best results from the lamps it is essential that they are in good alinement and that the bulbs are focused correctly.

Alternative positions are provided for the headlamp bulb in its holder. Each position should be tried for the best projection light.

To aline the lamps, slacken the single fixing nut, then move the lamp on its adjustable mounting to the desired position, finally locking the adjustment by tightening the nut.

Fuse. A fuse is provided with the electrical dipper unit to protect the equipment in the event of the reflector failing to function properly. The fuse is of the visible cartridge type, and is carried in spring clips alongside the dipping mechanism. If the reflector fails to function, remove the fuse from its holder and see whether there is a break in the fuse wire. A spare fuse is clipped to the reflector bracket.

Side Lamps. The side lamp fronts can be removed by twisting them to the left and withdrawing.

Stop and Tail Lamp. The back of the stop and tail lamp can be removed for bulb replacement by turning it to the left and withdrawing it from its base, when the fixing screw is slackened.

Bulb Sizes. The sizes of the bulbs are: Head, 618 S.V.; Side, B.A.S. No 8S; Tail, B.A.S. No. 8S; Stop, B.A.S. No. 8S; Dash, B.A.S. No. 8S.

The Reflectors. The reflectors of the lamps are covered with a

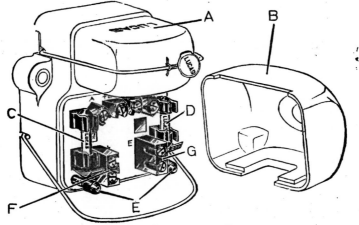

Fig. 71. Cut-out and Fuse

protective coating, and any marks can be easily removed with a soft cloth. On no account use any metal polish on reflectors.

The lighting and starting units on the Austin Seven are arranged for wiring on the earth return system so that it is essential that all units are in metallic contact with the frame.

Dynamo. The dynamo is a simple self-regulating third-brush machine. The only parts calling for any attention are the commutator and the brushes, which are readily accessible when the cover is removed. The commutator surface must be kept clean and free from any oil or brush dust. It may be cleaned with ordinary soft rag, but if it has been neglected use fine glass-paper. Blow away any carbon dust and see that the carbon brushes are wearing evenly and that the arms move freely on their pivots. To fit a new brush, it is only necessary to remove the single screw to withdraw the worn brush from its holder.

The dynamo bearings are packed with grease before leaving the works and do not require oiling.

Dynamo Field Fuse. A fuse is provided in the dynamo field circuit to protect the machine in the event of anything being wrong in the charging circuit, such as a loose or broken battery connection. The fuse is of the cartridge type and is housed with the half-charge resistance in the cut-out and fuse unit on the engine side of the dash (see Fig. 71). If the dynamo fails to charge the battery at any time (indicated by a discharge reading being given on the ammeter during day-time running) inspect the fuse, and if it has blown, replace it with the spare fuse provided, after inspecting the charging circuit wiring for loose or broken connections and remedying. This fuse must not be replaced while the engine is running. If the new fuse blows after starting up, the cause of the trouble must be found and remedied. Never fit any fuse other than the Lucas standard fuse as originally fitted. The size of the fuse is marked on a coloured paper slip which can be seen inside the fuse.

Starter Motor. The commutator of the starter motor is accessible on removing the sheet metal band cover. The unit requires very little attention beyond keeping the commutator clean and free from oil, brush dust, etc., as in the case of the dynamo. Remember that although the starter will turn the engine over, however stiff, it is advisable to crank the engine over by hand two or three revolutions, as this will considerably diminish the load for starting. This, of course, is only necessary when the car has been standing for some time.

If the starter pinion jams in mesh with the flywheel ring when operating the starter motor switch, usually it can be released by putting the gear lever into top gear, and moving the car bodily backwards and forwards. If this is not successful the starter will have to be dismantled.

Never use the starter motor to propel the car, as it throws too severe a strain on the battery and the motor.

If the engine does not start at the first attempt, do not press the starter switch until the engine has come to rest. If this precaution is not adopted, the starter ring teeth on the flywheel, or the starter pinion teeth, may be damaged.

Lighting and Charging Switch and Ignition Key. A key is provided by means of which the ignition switch is locked, so that the engine cannot be started. When the slot into which the key fits is in a vertical position, a spring releases the key and it may be withdrawn. The ignition is then cut off. To switch on the ignition, insert the key and turn to the right (clockwise), until the slot is in a horizontal line. The key cannot be withdrawn while the ignition is switched on; it must be turned off and the slot be in a vertical position first.

The lighting and charging switch positions (Fig. 72) are—

"Summer Half Charge" .	Dynamo giving about half its normal output.
"Winter Full Charge" .	Dynamo giving its full output.
"Side" . . .	Side lamps and tail lamp on.
"Head" . .	Head lamps, side lamps, and tail lamp on.

The dynamo automatically gives its full output when all the lamps are switched on.

Dipper Switch. If the headlights are on full, a touch of the left foot on the switch (Fig. 73) alters the lights to the "dip-and-switch" position, and they remain so until another touch returns them to the "full on" position.

Ammeter. The ammeter indicates the rate at which the battery is being charged or discharged.

FIG. 72. THE LIGHTING AND CHARGING SWITCH
AND IGNITION KEY

The ammeter gives an indication that the system is functioning satisfactorily. For example, if no reading is given on the charge side of the scale when the ignition and charging switch is in the "Winter Full C" position and the car is running at, say, 20 m.p.h. with lights off, then a fault in the dynamo charging circuit is indicated.

To determine the output of the dynamo, switch off all the lights and add the amount of current used for ignition (about 2 amp. at normal speeds) to the reading given on the ammeter.

The amount of current used for ignition may be somewhat higher than the above figure when starting. The ammeter does not indicate the amount of current used by the starter.

Cut-out and Fuse. The cut-out is mounted together with two fuses as one unit, which also forms a junction box and incorporates the half-charge resistance for the dynamo. The cut-out automatically closes the charging circuit as soon as the dynamo voltage rises sufficiently above that of the battery. When the dynamo voltage falls below that of the battery, the reverse action takes place, the cut-out opens and thereby prevents the battery from discharging itself through the dynamo.

The cut-out is accurately set before leaving the works, and does not need any adjustment and is therefore sealed.

The two fuses are of the cartridge type. The one marked "AUX" is connected to the accessories circuits, and will blow in the event of a short circuit in the wiring of the electric horn, windscreen wiper, and other units connected to the "AUX" terminal (see Fig. 70), the indication that the fuse has blown being the failure of these units.

The other fuse marked "DYN" protects the dynamo, and is

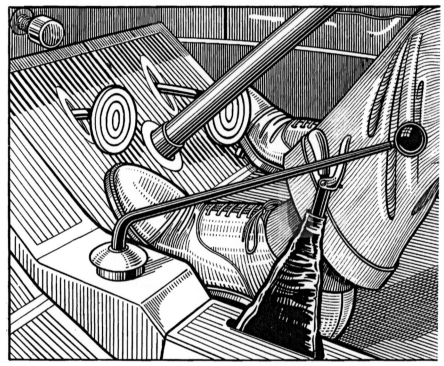

FIG. 73. THE HEADLIGHTS ARE DIPPED BY A TOUCH OF THE CONTROL ABOVE THE CLUTCH PEDAL

connected in the dynamo main circuit. The indication of a blown dynamo fuse is that the dynamo will fail to charge, no charge reading being given on the ammeter under normal day-time running conditions. Spare fuses are provided in cases of emergency. Before fitting a replacement fuse, examine the wiring of the equipment the fuse protects for loose connections or short circuits, and remedy.

Never fit any fuse other than the standard Lucas fuse as originally fitted.

Battery. It is of the utmost importance that the battery receives regular attention, as upon its good condition depends the satisfactory running of the starter motor, the functioning of the ignition, and the illumination of the lamps.

At least once a month the vent plugs in the top of the battery should be removed and the level of the acid solution examined. If necessary, distilled water, which can be obtained at all chemists and most garages, should be added to bring the level up to the top of the separators. If, however, acid solution has been spilled it should be replaced by a diluted sulphuric acid solution of 1·300 specific gravity. It is important when examining the cells that naked lights should not be held near the vents on account of the possible danger of igniting the gas coming from the plates. It is advisable to complete the inspection by measuring the specific gravity of the acid with a hydrometer as this gives a direct indication of the state of charge of the battery.

Charging Switch. The charging switch should be kept at the position appropriate to the season. For cars running under average conditions this will ensure that the battery is kept in condition without being overcharged. However, in some circumstances, it may be advisable to use the switch out of season. Thus, if in winter the car is run regularly during the day with practically no night running, resulting in the battery always being fully charged (hydrometer reading 1·285 or over), the switch should be kept in the "Summer Half Charge" position when the engine is running. Or, conversely, if exceptional use of the starter and lamps is made in the summer, causing the battery to be continuously in a low state of charge (hydrometer readings of 1·200 or under), the switch should be kept at the "Winter Full Charge" position while the engine is running.

On a new car, during the running-in period, it is advisable to keep the switch in the full charge position all the time in order to compensate for the heavy starter motor load due to the initial stiffness of the engine.

Should the state of the battery be continually bad, see that all its connections through the starter switch to the switchboard are tight and unbroken, and that no wire has a chafed covering, allowing leakage of current to the frame.

The Electrolyte. When the battery arrives empty (as in the case of cars sent abroad) the first thing to do is to fill and charge it.

This means that a solution is prepared composed of one part (by volume) of pure concentrated sulphuric acid with three parts (by volume) of distilled water. Mix these in a glazed earthenware vessel. Great care must be taken in this operation. Add the acid in very small quantities, almost drop by drop, and stir with a glass rod. *Never add the water to the acid.* This is highly dangerous and a serious explosion may result. This mixing generates heat, and it is important that the electrolyte should not be used in the battery before it has been allowed to cool. Pour the electrolyte into the cells of the battery by means of a glass or celluloid funnel, until it completely fills the cells to the top of the vent hole. Allow the battery to stand for 10 minutes or so, then put in more acid solution so that each cell is again filled to the same point with electrolyte. The electrolyte will have a specific gravity of 1·285 when fully charged. Batteries may be charged at almost any service station.

Direction Indicators. Every two or three months, raise the indicator arm and apply one drop of thin machine oil to the two hinged joints between the arm and the operating mechanism. Only the merest drop of oil should be added; any excess may affect the working of the solenoid mechanism.

If at any time, the arm fails to light up when in operation, examine the bulb. To remove the bulb, switch the indicator on, and then, supporting the arm in a horizontal position, move the switch to the "off" position.

Now withdraw the bulb holder, which is clipped into the underside of the arm, by means of the metal tongue provided. Do not attempt to remove the bulb holder while the indicator is switched on as this may cause a short circuit and so damage it.

On some models, move aside the small trigger projecting from the underside of the arm when the cap of the bulb holder will spring open. Fit a new bulb in place of the one which has burnt out and refit the cover.

Bulbs fitted: No. T63F, 3-watt festoon type.

If the direction indicators or electric petrol gauge fail to function examine the fuse protecting them (this is fitted on the dash near the cut-out); if it has blown, inspect the wiring for a short circuit.

The Electric Petrol Gauge. The electric petrol gauge is automatic in action and registers the contents of the petrol tank. It is active only when the ignition is switched on, consequently when the tank is being replenished, first switch off the ignition to stop the engine, then switch on again and the needle on the dial will record the amount of spirit which is poured into the tank.

There are four points at which a loose or broken connection might put the gauge out of action, these being, one at the tank unit and three at the back of the gauge, as will be seen from Fig. 74.

It is important that both the gauge and the tank unit should earth properly. The cable from the tank unit may be earthing at some point if the gauge shows a full tank without cause. I it

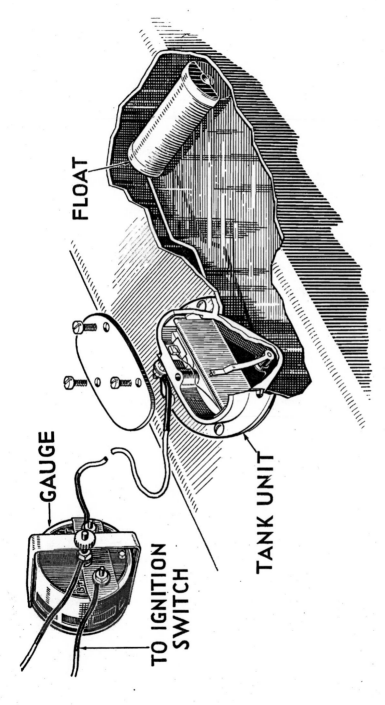

FLOAT

GAUGE

TO IGNITION SWITCH

TANK UNIT

FIG. 74. ARRANGEMENT OF THE WIRING FOR THE ELECTRIC PETROL GAUGE

is the tank unit terminal which is earthed, the unit will require repairing.

The gauge can be tested by connecting a voltmeter between the feed terminal *BX* and the battery positive terminal, having the battery negative connected up to the casing of the gauge. The battery negative can also be connected to the terminal *T* for the tank unit cable.

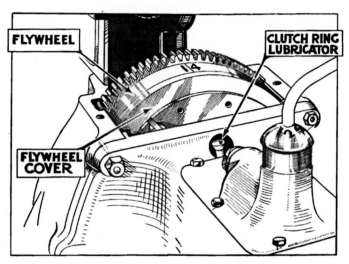

FIG. 75. RETIMING THE IGNITION

Another method is to use a voltmeter to test the tank unit, which should give slightly increased readings as the float arm is lifted by hand.

Electric Horn. These horns, before being passed out of the works, are adjusted to give their best performance, and will give a long period of service without any attention.

If the horn becomes uncertain in its action, giving only a choking sound, or does not vibrate, it does not follow that the horn has broken down. First ascertain that the trouble is not due to some outside source, e.g. a discharged battery, a loose connection or short circuit in the wiring of the horn, or a blown fuse.

It is also possible that the performance of a horn may be upset by the horn becoming loose on its mounting.

This can be ascertained by removing the horn from its mounting, holding it in the hand and pressing the push.

Electric Windscreen Wiper. To start, pull out the curved handle and swing it aside so as to move the cleaning arm into position on the screen. Then pull out the switch knob and give it a spin. To stop the wiper, push in the knob. Then pull out the curved handle and turn in to the top of the switch knob. This locks the arm out of the line of vision of the driver and also ensures that the wiper is switched off.

The wiper requires no attention; all the moving parts are packed with grease during assembly and no lubrication is required.

When cleaning the windscreen, the wiper arm can be easily lifted from the screen, but care must be taken that it is not forced from side to side.

Retiming the Ignition. To retime the ignition remove all the sparking plugs, except the front—No. 1—and turn the crankshaft by the starting handle until compression is felt.

Now turn the flywheel until the 1/4 line is $1\frac{1}{4}$ in. to 2 in. (see Fig. 75) before the top centre, and remove the distributor cover. The small screw on the clip fixing the control arm to the distributor casing is then slackened, the clip being kept at the full advanced position, and the casing turned anti-clockwise until the contact breaker points just begin to open. Then re-tighten the screw.

If after this the ignition seems too much or too little advanced, it can be adjusted by loosening the clamping screw of the control clip, and moving the casing relative to the clip a slight amount, anti-clockwise to advance the timing, or clockwise to retard. If the leads from the distributor have been disconnected for any purpose, they must be replaced correctly in the firing order marked on the distributor cover, thus: 1, 3, 4, 2.

Condition	Method of Detection of Possible Causes	Remedy
	Starter will not turn engine and lamps do not give good light. Battery discharged.	Start engine by hand. Battery should be recharged by running car for a long period during daytime with charging switch in full charge position. Alternatively recharge from an independent electrical supply.
	Controls not set correctly for starting.	See that ignition is switched on, petrol turned on, and everything is in order for starting.
Engine will not fire.	Remove lead from centre distributor terminal and hold it about ½ in. away from some metal part of the chassis, while engine is turned over. If sparks jump gap regularly, the coil and distributor are functioning correctly. If the coil does not spark, the trouble may be due to any of the following causes—	Examine the sparking plugs, and if these are clean and the gaps correct, the trouble is due to carburettor, petrol supply, etc.
	Fault in low tension wiring. Indicated by (1) No ammeter reading when engine is slowly turned and ignition switch is on, or (2) No spark occurs between the contact points when quickly separated by the fingers when the ignition switch is on.	Examine all cables in ignition circuit and see that all connections are tight. See that battery terminals are secure.
	Dirty or pitted contact points.	Clean with fine emery cloth and afterwards with a cloth moistened with petrol.
	Contact breaker points out of adjustment. Turn engine until contacts are fully opened and test gap with gauge and spanner.	Adjust gap to gauge.
	Dirty or pitted contact points.	Clean with fine emery cloth and afterwards with a cloth moistened with petrol.
Engine misfires.	Contact breaker points out of adjustment. Turn engine until contacts are fully opened and test gap with gauge and spanner.	Adjust gap to gauge.
	Remove each sparking plug in turn, rest it on the cylinder head, and observe whether a spark occurs at the points when the engine is turned. Irregular sparking may be due to dirty plugs or defective high tension cables. If sparking is regular at all plugs the trouble is probably due to engine defects.	Clean plugs and adjust the gaps to about 20 thousandths of an inch. Replace any lead if the insulation shows signs of deterioration or cracking. Examine carburettor, petrol supply, etc.

HOW TO LOCATE AND REMEDY DYNAMO TROUBLE

Symptoms	Probable Fault	Remedy
Ammeter fails to indicate charge when running with no lights in use, or gives heavy discharge with lights on.	Dynamo not charging due to: Broken or loose connection in charging circuit causing field fuse to blow. (When fitted.)	Examine charging circuit wiring. Tighten loose connection or replace broken lead. Particularly examine battery connections. Fit replacement fuse.
	Commutator greasy or dirty.	Clean with soft rag moistened in petrol.
	Dynamo giving low or intermittent output, due to—	
Ammeter gives low or intermittent charge reading.	Loose or broken connections in dynamo circuit.	Examine charging circuit wiring. Tighten loose connections or replace broken lead. Particularly examine battery connections.
	Commutator or brushes greasy.	Clean.
	Brushes worn, not fitted correctly, or wrong type.	Replace worn brushes. See that brushes "bed" correctly.
	Dynamo giving high output due to—	
	Loose connections in dynamo charging circuit.	Examine charging circuit wiring. Particularly battery connections. Tighten loose connections.
Ammeter gives high charge reading.	Battery acid level low.	"Top-up" cells with distilled water.
	Brushes not fitted correctly.	See that brushes "bed" correctly.
	Control brush position altered.	Have control brush adjustment reset at nearest Service Depot.

HOW TO LOCATE AND REMEDY STARTER MOTOR TROUBLE

Condition	Probable Fault	Remedy
	If engine cannot be turned by hand, then fault is due to a stiff engine.	Locate and remedy cause of stiffness.
	If engine can be turned by hand, then trouble may be due to—	
	Battery discharged.	Start by hand. Charge battery either by a long period of daytime running or from independent electrical supply.
Motor sluggish or fails to move engine.	Broken or loose connection in starter circuit.	See that connections to battery, starter, and starter switch are tight, and that cables connecting these units are in order.
	Starter commutator or brushes dirty.	Clean.
	Brushes worn, not fitted correctly or wrong type.	Replace worn brushes. See that brushes "bed" correctly.
	Starter pinion jammed in mesh with flywheel.	Rotate squared end of starter shaft with spanner. When a squared end is not provided on the starter shaft, the pinion can usually be released by putting the car in gear and rocking it backward and forward. If this method fails, remove starter from car and test its alinement. Remount starter and tighten fixing bolts.
Starter operates but does not crank engine.	Pinion of starter drive does not engage with flywheel, due to dirt on screwed sleeve.	Clean sleeve with paraffin and add a few drops of machine oil.
Starter pinion will not disengage from flywheel when engine is running.	Starter pinion jammed in mesh with flywheel.	Rotate squared end of starter shaft with spanner.

HOW TO LOCATE AND REMEDY LIGHTING TROUBLE

Symptoms	Probable Fault	Remedy
	Battery discharged.	Charge battery either by a long period of daytime running or from independent electrical supply.
Lamps give insufficient illumination.	Lamps out of alinement or bulbs out of focus.	Aline lamps and focus bulbs.
	Bulbs discoloured through use, or reflectors dirty.	Fit new bulbs or clean reflectors.
Lamps light when switched on, but gradually fade out.	Battery discharged.	As above.
Brilliance varies with speed of car.	Battery discharged.	As above.
	Battery connection loose or broken.	Tighten connections, or replace faulty cables.
Lights flicker.	Loose connection.	Locate loose connection and tighten.
Failure of lights.	Fuse blown.	Examine wiring for faulty cables and remedy. Fit replacement fuse.
	Battery discharged.	As above.
	Loose or broken connections.	Locate and tighten loose connection, or remake broken connection.

CHAPTER VIII

THE NEW CAR

THE first desire of the owner of a new Austin Seven upon taking delivery is almost always to gaze on it with admiration, to show it to all those interested friends, and to compare its performance with that of the car it supersedes, particularly so, if its predecessor was also a Seven. This desire, or combination of desires, should be curbed, and the owner's first responsibilities undertaken in a systematic and organized manner.

First of all, the driver's licence will be assumed to be in existence; then the insurance of the new car must be effected and registration duly accomplished. With all this clerical work, the warranty must not be overlooked. Fill in all the particulars required on the Warranty Form and send it to the Austin Motor Company Limited, at Longbridge, Birmingham, so that it can be registered there and the guarantee confirmed.

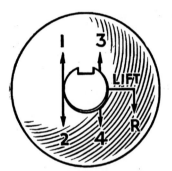

FIG. 76. GEAR LEVER POSITIONS

Then the elbows can be squared and the tools in the big sealed cardboard box checked against the tools list in either the handbook or spare parts book supplied with the car, or the list printed in this book on page 28. The small tools are kept in a pocketed wallet and the larger tools in separate wraps. This done, a general examination of the car can be undertaken with that keen relish peculiar to the motorist taking over a new car. The decision that everything is O.K. is the signal for the start of the first run.

Owners possessing a partiality for a running-in compound, especially a compound containing graphite in colloidal form, are strongly advised to use it, inserting it into the sump according to the makers' instructions.

First see that the supplies of petrol, water and oil are adequate, then see that the gear lever is in neutral (see Fig. 76). The controls and instruments can be clearly seen in Fig. 77. To start the engine turn the ignition switch key to the "on" position (9). Pull out the strangler (15), and then the pull-out starter switch (6).

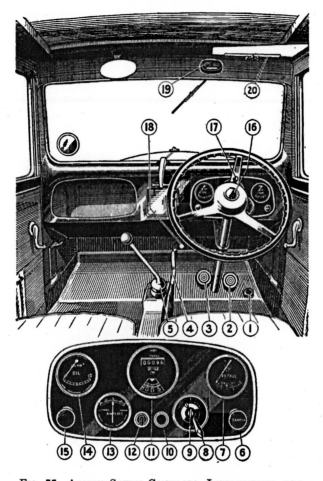

FIG. 77. AUSTIN SEVEN CONTROLS, INSTRUMENTS, ETC.

1 = Accelerator pedal
2 = Brake pedal
3 = Clutch pedal
4 = Hand brake lever
5 = Change speed lever
6 = Starter switch
7 = Petrol gauge
8 = Lighting and charging switch
9 = Ignition key
10 = Warning light
11 = Speedometer
12 = Dash light switch
13 = Ammeter
14 = Oil pressure gauge
15 = Carburettor strangler
16 = Horn button
17 = Direction indicator switch
18 = Dip-and-switch control
19 = Windscreen wiper
20 = Sun visor

Do not show off your car's paces to your friends however strong may be the urge. Restraint in this respect is vital to the service eventually to be given by your car. A new car must be run in carefully during the first 500 miles, and even afterwards, for reasons fully explained in the chapter on Lubrication.

The first attentions to the car should include running over all the accessible nuts and bolts with suitable spanners. This attention is particularly necessary for the cylinder-head and manifold nuts. The engine parts settle down with use and the heat from the functioning of the engine. This early attention will allow this slack to be taken up to maintain the efficiency of the car as a whole, as the running-in process proceeds.

The completion of the first 1,000 miles entitles the owner to take his car to his agent or to the Service Department at Long-bridge for it to undergo the after-sale inspection and tuning service which is provided free of charge.

With this important milestone in the life of the new Austin Seven safely passed, the owner can rest assured that, given proper care and attention, his car will provide him with many thousands of miles of care-free, dependable motoring.

CHAPTER IX

LAW FOR THE MOTORIST

IGNORANCE is no defence in Law.

The new motorist, and also those more mature, must acquire a smattering of the "do's" and "don'ts" necessary to conform to the requirements of the law.

The Road Traffic Act of 1930 is the principal Act affecting the motorist; it contains 123 Clauses and five schedules with numerous additional "Orders and Regulations."

Further to this Act is the Road and Rail Traffic Act of 1933 and the Road Traffic Act of 1934 with its Speed Limits in built-up areas and driving tests for applicants for new driving licences. This act contains many new regulations and many further amendments to old ones.

Also there are numerous other Acts, affecting the motorist, going back as far as the Highways Act of 1835, including the Petroleum Act of 1928 and the Road Transport Lighting Act of 1927. This survey will no doubt be frightening and bewildering to the new motorist, but it should not be difficult for him to assimilate the most important essentials among all the regulations affecting his use of a motor vehicle on the public highway. Motorists should not forget that membership of either the Royal Automobile Club of Pall Mall, London, S.W.1, or the Automobile Association of Fanum House, New Coventry Street, London, W.1, includes free legal defence in case of accident or police prosecution.

Every car must be fitted with number plates of a standard size at front and rear. The numbers must be kept clean and the rear one illuminated at night. The letters and digits on the number plate must be white on a black background and must conform with those written on the car licence, which latter must face forward or to the nearside and must be fitted in a suitable holder. The licence must also not be farther back than the front seat.

The tyres and brakes must be maintained in good and efficient order and the latter kept properly adjusted.

The horn must not be sounded between the hours of 11.30 p.m. and 7.30 a.m., or when the car is stationary except when waiting in traffic or when necessitated by reasons of safety (it is thus even unwise to summon the attendant at a petrol station by means of the horn).

Every car must be fitted with a reflecting mirror. No car may

123

emit excessive smoke. No person may use or give permission for the use of a car which is noisy from causes such as incorrect adjustment, lack of repair or faulty construction.

A tow rope used for towing must not be longer than 5 yards and must be easily visible to other road users.

No driver may drive his car in such a way as to endanger any member of the public or other road user. No car may be driven on a public road without two white lights to the front and one red one to the rear between one hour after sunset and one hour before sunrise. The front ones must also indicate the width of the car. No car may be left in a thoroughfare so as to cause unnecessary obstruction or left without applying the brakes.

The exhaust gases must not be allowed to escape into the atmosphere without first passing through an efficient silencer.

No car may be driven on the public roads without wings or sufficient protection from the car body; or driven beyond 15 yards on the common or moorland or land forming part of a footway or road.

If involved in an accident immediately notify the police and take the names and addresses of any independent witnesses. In the event of anyone being injured first obtain medical assistance. The driver should then immediately notify his insurance company and his motoring organizations.

On 18th March, 1935, Part I of the Road Traffic Act, 1934, came into force. This provides that "it shall not be lawful for any person to drive a motor vehicle on a road in a built-up area at a speed exceeding 30 miles per hour."

A built-up area is where "a system of street lighting is furnished by means of lamps placed not more than 200 yards apart." Some of the London by-passes and arterial roads are exempt from this part of the Act.

Driving Licence. Before any individual can drive a car he must obtain a driving licence. To obtain this fill in form D.L.1, which is obtained from any post office, and post it to the local authorities. No person under 17 years of age is allowed to drive a car.

The driving licence costs 5s. and is not granted to persons who have not already held a licence unless they pass a driving test.*
Learners can obtain a provisional licence (valid for three months) to enable them to obtain instruction pending the official test.

The learner, when obtaining his or her instruction with a provisional licence, must carry an "L" plate at both front and rear of his car and also be accompanied by a person who has held a licence for at least two years.

When the learner considers that the necessary proficiency in driving has been obtained he may apply for his test. To do this

* *Your Driving Test: How to Pass It* (Stewart). Pitman, 2s. net.

he must fill in form D.L.26, obtainable from the local motor
taxation office. Fill it in, and send it, together with the necessary
7s. 6d. to the Supervizing Examiner for the district.

If the applicant successfully passes the tests he will be author-
ized to take out a proper annual driving licence. The applicant
can undertake another test a month later if at first he is unsuccess-
ful. There is no limit to the number of tests the novice may
undertake.

When the licence or its renewal is obtained it must be ensured
that the holder's signature is affixed.

To pass the driving tests mentioned the novice is expected to
be quite *au fait* with the contents of the Highway Code (obtainable
from H.M. Stationery Office or the local taxation offices, price 1d.),
and be able to read a number plate possessing six characters at a
distance of 25 yards in good daylight and with glasses, if worn.

He must also be able to start the engine of his Seven and move
straight ahead or at an angle; overtake, meet or cross the path
of other vehicles and take an appropriate course. Turn right- and
left-hand corners correctly; stop the car in an emergency, and
normally, and in the latter case stop it at an appropriate part of
the road.

He must be able to (1) drive backwards and enter a limited
opening either to the right or to the left. (2) Turn the Seven
round so as to face in the opposite direction by using both forward
and reverse gears. (3) Give by hand or mechanical means, clear,
definite, and unmistakable signals at appropriate times to indicate
his intended actions. (4) Act correctly and promptly on all signals
given by traffic signs and controllers and take appropriate action
on signs given by other road users.

In all, he must convince his examiner that he is fully competent
to drive a motor vehicle.

Any person driving a motor-car must on the demand of a
police officer, produce his driving licence for examination. or
produce it personally within five days at a police station specified
by him at the time.

If involved in an accident, however, remember that only 24
hours is allowed for the driver to report it to the police.

A conviction in connexion with a motoring offence may involve
the disqualification from holding or obtaining a driving licence.
Appeal from such disqualification can be made by the driver
before the Court before which he was convicted. not earlier than
six months from the date of conviction.

Any disqualification is endorsed on the driving licence, and
on subsequent licences unless in the meantime the driver has
become entitled to have a licence issued to him free from endorsement. Freedom from endorsement is granted at the expiration

of a period of three years, provided that no further order has been made, and subject to payment of a fee of 5s. and to the surrender of any existing licence.

Any driver who is disqualified and obtains a licence, or drives another vehicle is liable on conviction to imprisonment for a term not exceeding six months ; or a fine not exceeding £50, or both.

If a driving licence is lost a duplicate can be obtained from the local taxation office for a fee of one shilling.

Insurance. All motorists must insure against third party claims for personal injury and a certificate of insurance from the company has to be produced to the taxation authorities before a Road Fund licence can be obtained.

The usual third party insurance covers damage to other people's property as well as any liability that may be incurred in respect of the death of, or bodily injury to, any person caused by the use of the insured vehicle on the road. Most people favour the additional security afforded by a fully comprehensive policy which covers any damage to their car as well as other risks. Full details of the "cover" afforded by the different insurance companies can be obtained from their literature. Cheap insurance may not always turn out cheap when claims are settled.

A considerable percentage of the premium can be saved by the careful driver in "No claim bonus" for each year clear of claims.

Like the driver's licence the certificate of insurance must be available for police inspection if required or alternatively produced within five days at a specified police station.

Registration. The motor agent from whom the new Seven is purchased will see to all the formalities necessary when first registering a new car. The tax is £6 a year and can be taken from any day in the year for its remainder at a proportion of the full annual tax. Fourteen days' grace are allowed for renewal. Before the end of this period, if it is desired to renew the licence, the renewal form R.F. 1 A. must be carefully completed from the information contained in the registration book and sent together with the necessary remittance, the certificate of insurance, and the registration book, to the taxation authorities. Any change in the specification of the car should be notified to the authorities when renewing a Road Fund Licence. If renewal is obtained from a Post Office the old licence will also have to be enclosed.

CHAPTER X

THE BIG SEVEN

A RECENT addition to the range is the Big Seven, and the specification and maintenance details are given below.

This entirely new model supplements the Austin range as an enlarged version of the famous Austin Seven. It has a four-door six-light or two-door four-light saloon body, a new chassis and power unit, with "live" rubber engine mountings, low periodicity springing and full Girling brakes. The bodywork is particularly generously equipped, with large-dial instruments and a rear panel that encloses the spare wheel or serves as a luggage platform. The specification also includes compensated voltage control and the new engine, which has inclined valves and a three-bearing counterbalanced crankshaft, develops 25 b.h.p. at 4000 r.p.m., although only rated at 7·992 h.p. and carrying £6 tax.

The general maintenance instructions given for t'₂ Seven apply in the main to the Big Seven also. The purpose of this chapter is thus to provide additional information where required by differences in design.

GENERAL SPECIFICATION OF THE AUSTIN BIG SEVEN

Engine. 4-cylinder monobloc with cylinders and crankcase one casting; detachable head and sump; bore 56·77 mm., stroke 88·9 mm., cubic capacity 900 c.c.; R.A.C. rating 7·992 h.p.; 25 b.h.p. at 4000 r.p.m.; side valves; aluminium alloy pistons; three-bearing counterbalanced crankshaft; coil ignition, with automatic advance; thermo-siphon cooling with fan; forced lubrication; downdraught carburettor with air silencer; pump fuel feed from 6-gal. rear tank.

Transmission. Improved single-plate clutch with flexible centre and spring drive; four-speed gearbox, ratios 22·39, 13·52, 8·52, 5·125 to 1; syncromesh engagement for second, third and top; Hardy-Spicer propeller shaft; ¾-floating rear axle.

Frame. Of special triangular design, with deep inverted U-section side-members.

Suspension. Semi-elliptic transverse front spring, and quarter-elliptic rear springs; large friction shock-absorbers.

Brakes. Girling mechanical, applied by hand and pedal on all four wheels.

Wheels and Tyres. "Easy-clean" pressed-steel spoke wheels with large centres. Dunlop extra low pressure tyres, 4·75–16.

Fig. 78. The " Big Seven " Four-light Saloon

Steering. Hour-glass type worm-and-sector.

Electrical Equipment. 6-volt starting, lighting, and ignition. Foot controlled dip-and-switch headlamps; stop-and-tail lamp; large dial instruments with concealed lighting; petrol gauge; high frequency horn; automatic-return direction indicators; windscreen wiper; compensated voltage control.

Other Equipment. Bumpers front and rear; interior visor; driving mirror; magnetic speedometer; draught and fume excluders and ventilators; luggage platform; enclosed spare wheel and tyre; Triplex toughened glass in screen and windows; sliding roof; best quality leather.

Dimensions. Wheelbase 7 ft. 3½ in.; track, front 3 ft. 7¼ in., rear 3 ft. 9 in.; overall length 11 ft. 2 in., overall width 4 ft. 6 in., overall height 5 ft. 5 in.; ground clearance 5¾ in.; turning circle 36 ft.

Regular Attentions

This is a handy summary of all the attentions necessary. The attentions under the daily, weekly and monthly headings are based on the assumption that the maximum mileage per week does not exceed 500 (800 km.).

Under more strenuous conditions, i.e. very dusty or very muddy roads, long distances at high speeds or with heavy loads, it will be advisable to attend to the lubrication of chassis parts more frequently.

After the first few days' use, tighten all nuts, particularly those on the engine cylinder head. These may become slack because of the heat generated, but if they are retightened the cylinder head will remain secure against gas or water leaks.

Warning. After the car has been washed, or driven through water, the brake linings may be wet. Apply the brakes a number of times for some distance in order to dry them. Wet brakes are dangerous. Keep the handbrake hard on when the car is being washed.

Every Day. 1. Examine water-level in radiator and fill-up to within 1 in. of the top.

2. Fill the petrol tank if necessary. The capacity is 6 gal. (26½ litres).

Every Week. (1) Examine oil level in the crankcase and add more oil if necessary.

The dip rod indicates the level of the oil. Change the oil first at 500 miles (800 km.), then every 2000 miles (3000 km.).

The sump capacity is 5 pints.

(2) With the grease gun charge—

Front spring shackle pins (4).

Front axle swivel pins (2).

Steering cross tube (2).

Steering side tube joints (2).

Rear spring pins (2).

(3) Oil the following—

Foot brake pedal shaft (below steering box).

Brake cross-shaft bearings (use a brush).

(4) Examine the brakes, and adjust if necessary.

(5) Test the tyres for correct pressure and examine them for cuts, flints and nails.

Every Month. (1) Examine the oil level in the gearbox. It should be level with the filler plug. Capacity, approximately 1¼ pints.

Change at first 1000 and then every 6000 miles.

(2) Charge the back axle case with special lubricant, using the adaptor on the grease gun. Capacity ⅞ pint.

Change at first 1000 and then every 6000 miles.

(3) Grease the hubs.

(4) Charge the steering box with special lubricant.

(5) Oil handbrake gear, pedal gear and joints, engine control joints, and top of steering column.

(6) Examine the battery, top up if necessary, and see that the connexions are tight. (More frequently in hot weather.)

(7) Give a few drops of oil to the distributor spindle bearing.

(8) Grease the front end of the torque tube (behind and beneath the front seats).

(9) Grease the splined end of the propeller shaft (behind the gearbox). Turn the shaft to expose the nipple.

OCCASIONAL ATTENTIONS

Clean the sparking plugs and check the gap settings.

Examine all bolts and nuts, such as road spring clips, cylinder-head nuts, wheel nuts, these three especially when the car is new.

Examine other parts, such as steering connexions, the radius rod and torque tube anchorages, neglect of which might be followed by an expensive repair and inability to use the car for a lengthy period.

Occasionally clean the pump and carburettor fuel filters and every 3000 miles the oil reservoir filter (when the engine oil is changed).

Flush the radiator with plenty of clean water until it runs through clear. Clean the ignition distributor, and the contact-breaker points (adjust the latter), the dynamo and starter commutators. Clean the shock absorbers, adjust the tappets, and the fan belt, decarbonize the engine and grind-in the valves. Check the alinement of the front wheels.

INSTRUMENTS

Fuel Gauge. The fuel gauge is electrically operated and automatically indicates the contents of the tank when the ignition control is switched on. The capacity is 6 gal. (26¼ litres).

Oil Gauge. The gauge may indicate a pressure of 35 lb. per sq. in. or more when the engine is cold or from 20 to 30 lbs. when hot. With the engine running at constant speed the needle should be quite steady.

Panel Lights. The instruments are illuminated by two lamps controlled by the same switch. The holders can be pulled from the back of the instruments to facilitate removal of the bulbs.

Switch Box. When the engine is not in use the ignition key should be withdrawn from the switch box. The red warning light indicates when the ignition is "on" and the battery is discharging through the coil.

The dynamo has compensated voltage control and the main switch only operates the lighting of the head and side lamps.

Tyres.

Tyre Size	Front Tyres	Rear Tyres	Fully Laden
4·75–16 E.L.P.	20 lb. per sq. in.	20 lb. per sq. in.	22 lb. per sq. in.

SPARKING PLUGS

The sparking plugs with which the "Big Seven" is fitted are 14 mm. K.L.G. type, L777.

The gaps between the firing point of the central electrode and the earth points are set at 0·015 in. to 0·018 in.

MAINTENANCE

Decarbonizing and Valve Grinding. See appropriate section in the book.

Clutch Wear Take-up. After the clutch has been in use for some time the wear of the friction surfaces will give rise to a need for adjustment in order to ensure the continued full engagement of the clutch.

The adjustment should be such as to allow at least ⅜ in. free movement of the clutch pedal with one finger.

The adjustment is obtained by slightly slackening the clamping screw at the bottom of the clutch pedal lever and depressing the pedal sufficiently to give the required free movement. The clamping screw must then be securely tightened and the adjustment checked.

Brake Adjustment. There is only one operation necessary at each wheel to adjust the brake shoes. This is as follows—

On the opposite side of the drum whence the operating rod protrudes will be seen the square-ended brake shoe adjuster. This can be turned a notch at a time, which can be felt and heard and is the engagement of the four flat sides of the cone on the inner end of the adjuster engaging with the plungers which support the shoes.

Screw the adjuster into its housing as far as it will go. The brake shoes are then hard on and the adjuster should be turned back three full notches to give the shoes the necessary clearance from the drum.

Each drum should be treated similarly. It is not necessary to jack up the wheels.

After adjustment is completed, press the brake pedal down as hard as possible once or twice in order to centralize the brake shoes in the drums.

The handbrake operates on all wheels, and it is important that no attempt should be made to adjust the brakes with the handbrake on.

On the rear brakes the adjuster will be found immediately in front of the axle.

Lubrication. It is important that the nipple on the brake balance lever near the centre of the rear axle be lubricated at least once a month. All brake joints should be oiled occasionally either by high pressure or with a brush.

The Carburettor. The carburettor fitted to the Austin Seven is of the Zenith downdraught type, embodying the well-known principles of main and compensating jets.

Standard Setting. Settings are likely to be varied to suit certain markets. Standard settings are—

Choke 23	Slow-running Jet . . 60
Main Jet . . . 90	Needle Seating . . 1·5 mm.
Compensating Jet . . 50	

Intake Silencer. An A.C. oil-wetted carburettor intake silencer and air-cleaner is fitted.

At frequent intervals, say weekly, where dust is constantly experienced, the silencer needs cleaning and re-oiling. It is pulled off from the carburettor and the top of the cleaner is swilled in a shallow pan of petrol.

After drying, the metal gauze mesh should be re-oiled with engine oil, allowing the surplus to drain off before refitting the cleaner.

If the air cleaner is neglected it becomes choked with dirt, so that the cleaning efficiency of the device and its valuable protection against engine wear are not maintained.

The Cooling System. The cooling of the engine is maintained by a capacious radiator which should be filled with rain water, if available, or clean soft water, up to within about 1 in. of the filler.

The capacity of the radiator, pipes and cylinder jacket is approximately 13 pints.

Fan Belt Adjustment. The fan belt should be adjusted so that it is not too taut but will not slip. To make the adjustment slacken the link locking nut at the front of the cylinder head and raise or lower the dynamo until the desired tension of the belt is obtained. Then securely lock the dynamo in position again.

The Electrical System. The electrical system on the Austin "Big Seven" is 6-volt and the positive pole of the batteries is earthed.

The Dynamo. The dynamo is specially designed to work in conjunction with a compensated voltage regulator unit, mounted on the engine side of the dash, which automatically controls the dynamo output to meet the varying requirements of the batteries and load.

When the batteries are discharged, the dynamo gives a high output so as to bring the batteries back to their normal fully charged state in the minimum time. When the batteries are fully charged, the dynamo only gives a trickle charge, which is sufficient to keep the batteries in good condition without possibility of damage through over-charging.

The dynamo gives an increase of output to balance the current taken by the lamps or other accessories when these are switched on.

The control of the dynamo output is entirely automatic. Hence there is no charging switch.

The only parts calling for any attention are the commutator and brushes, which are readily accessible when the cover is removed.

Cut-out and Regulator. The cut-out and regulator are mounted with two fuses as one unit, which also forms a junction box.

The working of the regulator in conjunction with the dynamo has already been described.

The function of the cut-out is to close the charging circuit as increasing engine speed causes the dynamo voltage to rise above that of the batteries. When the engine slows down the dynamo voltage falls below that of the battery and the reverse action takes place ; the cut-out opens and prevents the battery discharging through the dynamo.

The cut-out and regulator are set before leaving the works and *do not need adjustment.* The cover protecting them is sealed.

One fuse protects the accessories which are operative only when the ignition is switched on (e.g. fuel gauge, horn, stop lamp and direction indicators). The other fuse protects those accessories which can be operated irrespective of whether the ignition is on or off, including the interior light and the screen wiper.

If any of the units fail, inspect the fuse protecting them and if it has blown examine the wiring for a short circuit and remedy. If the new fuse blows, the cause of the trouble must be found, and we advise that the equipment is examined by an Austin dealer or a Lucas Service Depot.

Bulb Sizes.

Headlamp, Lucas No. 106.
Side, stop and tail lamps, Lucas No. 200.
Ignition warning lamp, Lucas No. C252 A.

NEW MOTORING LAWS

Lighting Regulations. All motor vehicles must comply with the Ministry of Transport Lighting Regulations. The most important clause deals with that bugbear of all night-driving motorists, viz. dazzle.

No lamp showing a light to the front shall be used unless such lamp is so constructed and fitted to the vehicle that the beam of light emitted therefrom—

(i) "is permanently deflected downwards to such an extent that it is at all times incapable of dazzling any person standing on the same horizontal plane as the vehicle at a greater distance than 25 ft. from the lamp, and whose eye-level is not less than 3 ft. 6 in. above that plane ; or

(ii) "can be deflected downwards or both downwards and to the left at the will of the driver in such manner as to render it incapable of dazzling any such person in the circumstances aforesaid ; or

(iii) "can be extinguished by the operation of a device which either deflects the beam of light from another lamp in accordance with sub-paragraph (ii) of this paragraph or brings into, or leaves in, operation a lamp or lamps (other than the obligatory front lamps) which comply with sub-paragraph (i) of this paragraph."

Another important clause is that every electric bulb showing a light to the front must have the wattages marked on it. Also, no electric bulb of a power exceeding 7 watts shall be kept illuminated while the vehicle is stationary on a road except during an enforced stoppage.

Brake Tests. The police have power to test the brakes, silencers, and steering on private premises if the owner consents or is notified that such test is to take place. Forty-eight hours' notice of the intended test must be given by the police. The notice does not apply in the case of a vehicle which has been involved in an accident within the previous forty-eight hours.

Mascots. A mascot must not be carried in a position where it is likely to strike any person in collision unless the mascot is of such a design that it is not likely to cause injury.

Windscreen Wipers. It is compulsory to have an efficient windscreen wiper fitted to every vehicle, unless, by opening the windscreen or otherwise, the driver can obtain an adequate view of the front of the vehicle without looking through the screen. The wiper must be kept in good working order and must be properly adjusted.

APPENDIX

THE Austin Seven of the present day is not vastly different, in point of design, from its predecessors of the past twelve years.

Radical changes in specification, purely for change's sake, are not favoured by the designers at Longbridge.

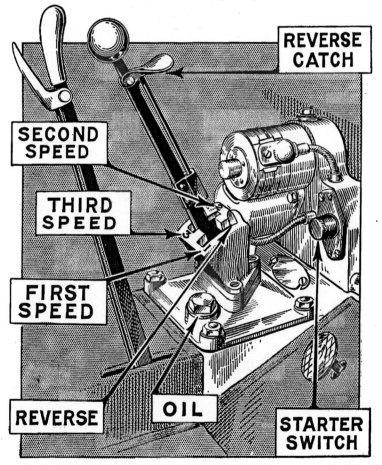

FIG. 78. THE THREE-SPEED GATE CHANGE GEARBOX WAS SUPERSEDED BY THE BALL CHANGE BOX IN OCTOBER, 1929

Alterations in design have been introduced as and when the circumstances have justified them; so maintaining a policy of constant improvement.

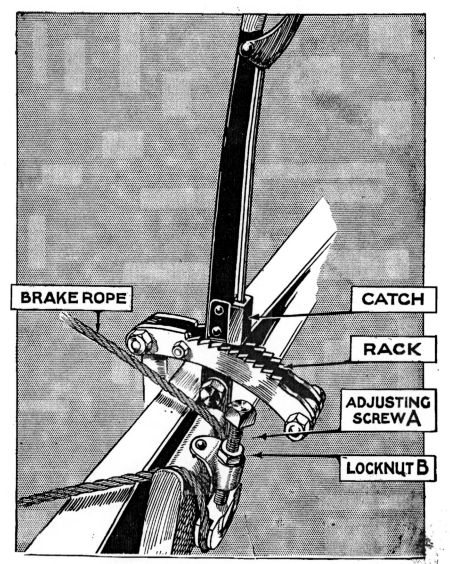

FIG. 79. SEPARATE HAND AND FOOT BRAKES WERE SUPERSEDED BY THE COUPLED SYSTEM IN JULY, 1930

FIG. 80. THE BATTERY ON THE STANDARD SEVEN WAS MOVED FROM UNDER THE PASSENGERS' SEAT AND LOCATED UNDER THE BONNET IN FRONT OF THE SCUTTLE IN AUGUST, 1934

The following list is a summary of various chassis features that have been introduced from time to time since 1927.

Year	Month	Chassis	Features Introduced
1927	Oct.	45,016	Speedometer drive from gearbox (BH 100).
	Dec.	50,901	Extensions on frame (BR 71).
1928	April	59,275	Starting handle bracket aluminium die cast (BD 17).
	July	65,442	Steering wheel with shallower dish and splined fixing (BM 126).
	Aug.	67,024	Raised radiator, cowl and bonnet (BD 101).
	Sept.	69,104	Coil ignition engine (BA 118).
	Dec.	73,933	Wide door metal saloon made standard.
1929	June	90,030	Front spring with 8 leaves (BR 79).
	Sept.	96,598	Wings with deep edge, without a mould.
	Oct.	99,001	Ball change speed lever (BH 113). Starter with switch (BG 124).
1930	Jan.	103,458	Wings with raised moulding.
	May	110,900	Dial type oil indicator (BG 138).
	July	113,000	Hand and foot controls coupled (BK 43, BN 48).
1931	March	130,000	Peg type starting handle (BD 200) and nut (BB 52).
1932	Oct.	159,534	Tank at rear (BE 112) 4-speed gearbox (BH 135).
			Starter on off-side of engine (BG 173).
			Combined induction and exhaust manifold (BE 117).

Year	Month	Chassis	Features Introduced
1932	Oct.	159,534	Petrol gauge on instrument panel (BG 168). Speedometer of moving figure pattern. Switchbox with ignition key (BG 160). Dashlamp embodied in instrument panel (BG 162). Wide brake drums (BL 71, BO 144). Spring type plated radiator cap (BD 224). Rear axle centre case in one piece with off-side tube (BO 143).
1933	June	176,687	Hardy Spicer rear universal joint (BP 126).
	Aug.	179,368	3rd and 4th Speed Synchromesh gearbox (BH 224).
1934	July	198,596	Needle type prop: shaft on Saloon (BP 161). Sloping cellulose cowl for saloon (BD 282).
	Aug.	198,678	2nd, 3rd, and 4th Speed Synchromesh gearbox (BH 297). Automatic ignition control. Trafficator switch on steering wheel (BM 183). Sloping cellulose cowl for Tourer (BD 282).
	Nov.	205,849	Ball bearing used on rear end of bevel pinion shaft replaced by roller bearing on larger diameter.
1935	Jan.	¹213,111	Peg-type valve spring cup fixing introduced.
	March	219,428	Radiator filler cap position changed to offside.
	April	220,395	Modified headlamps and cables in harness form, making lamps and wiring self-contained.
	July	226,847	Brake shoe leverage increased.
	Dec.	236,210	Electrical earthing circuit, positive pole earthed
1936	Feb.	¹241,541	"Nippy" Sports model fitted with faster "Speedy" engine with full pressure lubrication system.
	March	241,738	1st and 2nd speed fork rod modified.
	May	246,176	Cast iron brake drums introduced.
	June	246,835	Aluminium brake shoes replaced by steel shoes.
	June	¹249,001	Centre bearing for crankshaft.

¹ Engine No.

WAR-TIME REGULATIONS

Lighting Restrictions. If you propose to drive during black-out hours you must have a mask fitted to one of your head lamps, and it is advisable to purchase one of the officially approved types. There are a number of these on the market and provided they are not tampered with you should be immune from police attention in this direction. The mask may be fitted to the near-side or off-side but not to both. The bulb must be removed from the one not being used. A headlamp mask must also be fitted in the case of a motor-cycle, and this must be a dual-purpose type.

During foggy weather it is permissible to use one of the head-lamps *unmasked*, provided (1) the lamp is operated by a separate switch; (2) the beam is directed downwards towards the near-side; (3) it is used only when fog conditions really demand it; and (4) it is immediately extinguished when an air-raid warning is given. Should a police officer not consider the fog dense enough to warrant the use of the unmasked lamp he has authority to order the light to be extinguished.

The bulb used in the side and rear lamps must not exceed 7 watts in power and the reflector must be painted black or rendered non-effective. Light may be emitted only through a single aperture facing to the front or rear as the case may be, of not more than 1 in. diameter. Side panels must be completely blacked-out. Also, the aperture through which the light is emitted must be partially obscured by placing behind the glass, paper or some such other uncoloured material having a density equal to that of two sheets of newspaper, or by applying a thin coat of paint to the interior of the glass in such a manner that approximately the same effect is produced. The paper, paint or whatever material is used must cover the whole of the portion of the front glass through which light can pass and must not be treated in any way to increase its transparency. Also, rear lamps must not be fitted at a greater height than 3 ft. 6 in., except in the case of certain public service vehicles.

Stoplights may be used provided they are so masked that the aperture through which light is emitted is of an area not exceeding 1 sq. in.; the aperture must also be treated in the same way as the side lamps. Reversing lamps are *not* allowed.

Interior illumination which can be seen from the exterior of the car is prohibited.

Direction indicators may still be used provided they too are blacked-out and here the law requires that the light shall be restricted to a small arrow-shaped window. The exact depth of this arrow must not be more than ½ in.

Anti Fifth-column Measures. When putting the vehicle away for the night the law demands that some action is taken to put it out of commission in order that it is not used by any unauthorized persons. In addition to the ignition key being removed and the doors locked, it is necessary to remove part of the mechanism.

Camouflage. This is not compulsory, but should you wish your vehicle to be camouflaged make sure you do not use any of the "Services" colour schemes.

Speed Limit. This is now fixed at 20 m.p.h. in built-up areas during the hours of black-out governed by lighting-up times.

Parking. It is compulsory to park your car or motor-cycle at the near-side of the road during black-out, and the lights must be left on. It is an offence to leave the headlamps switched on when the vehicle is stationary.

FUEL AND OIL
RUNNING EXPENSES

Date	PETROL		OIL		Speedo-meter Reading	M.P.G.	
	Gallons	£ s. d.	Pints	£ s. d.		Petrol	Oil

FUEL AND OIL
RUNNING EXPENSES

Date	PETROL		OIL		Speedo-meter Reading	M.P.G.	
	Gallons	£ s. d.	Pints	£ s. d.		Petrol	Oil

INDEX

Lightning Source UK Ltd.
Milton Keynes UK
UKOW04f1904191015

260948UK00001B/17/P